LEARN TO

LIVE

THE BOOK THAT CAN CHANGE YOUR LIFE

MATS & SUSAN BILLMARK

Inre Hälsa Förlag AB
Översättning: Lauren Chaleff and Dee Eckert Lundqvist
Coverphoto: Joachim Grusell
Back-cover photo: Julia Billmark
Cover design: Mathias Billmark and Julia Billmark

TABLE OF CONTENTS

To Julia
Our beloved daughter and source of inspiration.

FOREWORD

My dear friends, Mats and Susan asked me to read through this book, and I have enjoyed doing so thoroughly. I understand the struggle they have been through, and how their path back to happiness and harmony is a source of wisdom for us all. To show so much courage and meet themselves and each other and to be able to ask for help from other people shows great inner strength.

I know with certainty that many people will be helped and feel empowered to change their lives after sharing in Mats and Susan´s journey, and getting to listen to their innermost thoughts and reflections. It is therefore with great joy that I leave you to read this book and find the inspiration and strength Mats´ and Susan want to share with you.

Mikael Werthwein

AUTHORS

MATS BILLMARK

I was born in Kalmar, Sweden. My first job was my own startup. I have always been a leader and an entrepreneur. For years I hid my anxiety by being outgoing and having a friendly personality. I doubt very many people knew what a low self-esteem I had.

For the last few years I have focused my work on psychological illness, a topic that is very important to me. In 2011 my lecture "Inner health" premiered at a hotel in Kalmar, and the response was incredible. After six sold-out lectures in Kalmar I have travelled and lectured in numerous other cities. In 2013 I even released a DVD version of the "Inner Health" lecture series. My new focus these days is to live more present in the now. I am totally convinced that the basis for a more satisfying, happier, better life is conscious presence in the moment.

I am still quite sensitive to stress. For better or for worse I have finally realized that I will never have the same strength and energy that I had before my burnout and illness. Nowadays I have learned to know myself better and I know where my limits are.

SUSAN BILLMARK

I was born in Ludvika, Sweden. I was a very shy child but I was lucky enough to be surrounded by creative and extroverted peers. I learned from them to dare to do what I wanted to. I eventually overcame my shyness and learned how to step outside my comfort zone and become more confident. One thing led to another and I became a person with a lot on my plate. I had a hard time saying no, for fear that I would be disliked.

In hindsight, looking at my resulting exhaustion-depression, I realize that it takes a strong person to have such a dramatic breakdown as I did. I repressed my needs, and didn´t understand my own worth, or that I was important to take care of. Then, in the last few years I have rediscovered my creativity. I have learned how to strengthen it and make it a part of my everyday life. Intuitively I knew that creating things would make me healthy. And it did! Creativity has been so important for my rehabilitation. I wish I had realized this sooner. Now it is such a huge part of my life. I know it´s a great tool to improve the quality of life and of health. For this reason I´ve added a whole chapter on creativity.

These days my biggest challenges are my weight and my sugar cravings. I hate sweating and exercising, so losing weight is no easy task! For a long time, my body didn´t get the respect it deserves. Now I am prioritizing my body. I feel it´s especially important now that I´m past 50!

ABOUT US

We met in Kalmar in 1995. Mats was planning a big conference and needed a decorator. Since that time we have been inseparable, and have often worked together.

In May of 1996 our daughter Julia was born. In 2011 our family got even bigger when we were joined by two temporary foster children, Elsa (born 2004) and Martin (born 2009).

It´s hard to translate the Swedish foster care system into other countries, but to summarize: in Sweden there are some children who are still in their parents´custody, but who spend some time with "support families" in order to make things easier on their parents and for the child to experience a different way of living than they are used to. A way for the children to get more adult role models and broaden their contacts.

WHY WE WROTE THIS BOOK

Imagine if we had had this book when we were feeling so low! Well, here it is! We hope that it will help many people who, like us, don't realize that they need to stop what they are doing and reflect over the direction of their lives.

We didn´t have this book, but we had each other. At our worst, we didn´t always feel helped by one another but we always had support and someone who understood how challenging stress and anxiety can be. Our doctor advised us to write down our experiences, and we did, but we never planned to share them with anyone. Eventually a few of our friends read these journals and were deeply moved. We knew then that what we wrote could help people who had similar issues.

Our hope is that you will be able to stop yourself in time before your problem goes as far as ours did for us.

We recommend that you read this book slowly. Read a chapter, let the message sink in, and think about how it relates to your life. You can also focus on the chapters that resonate with you the most.

You can make a change for the better!

LIVING IN THE MOMENT

When the Dalai Lama was asked what surprised him most about humanity, he answered:

> *Man. Because he sacrifices his health in order to make money. Then he sacrifices money in order to recuperate his health. And then he is so anxious about the future that he does not enjoy the present; the result being that he does not live in the present or the future; he lives as if he is never going to die, then dies having never really lived.*

At least once, we have all felt that feeling when everything has fallen into place. For just a few moments, we experience a calm and inner peace where we want to remain. You know exactly what we mean – a few seconds of total and intense joy together with your child, your partner, or your pet. It could also be an amazing experience in nature.

If you know what we are talking about, you have had a little taste of total presence in the NOW!

Why, oh why do we have such a hard time living in the moment? Our brains are constantly thinking about the future and analyzing how what we do now will affect us later. We analyze the past and use that information to come up with new and creative ideas, insights, and solutions. That is why we are more busy and interested in the future and the past than the present.

The past defines us and gives us a sense of identity. The future always holds hope of success and happiness. But what about the present?

THAT CONSTANT CHATTER

We are obsessed with our thoughts. As soon as we wake up **the voice in our head** begins, and it doesn´t turn off until we fall asleep again. When we are stressed, we can barely manage to quiet our thoughts for ten seconds.

Intellect and thoughts are our biggest assets as humans, but when the noise in our heads takes over and we miss the chance to enjoy the moment, then our thoughts truly become a burden. We must strive to maintain a healthy balance between consciousness and awareness of the present, and thoughts about the past and future.

Many people don't even notice that they are actually thinking all the time, without interruption. The voice in their head comments, speculates, judges, compares, complains, dislikes, and likes etc. For many people, these thoughts are their main cause of stress, low self-esteem, unhappiness, and disappointment.

We always live in the present, but we rarely pay attention to it.

The constant buzz of thoughts in our heads makes it almost impossible.

> ***Mats Tells a Story:***
> *I remember one experience that really made me aware of how overactive our thoughts are. It happened in the grocery store. A man was walking up and down the aisles talking to himself about all kinds of things – what he was going to eat for dinner, and what he would say in a phone call later. How did the other people in the store react? They went out of their way to avoid this man with the strange behavior. Then it struck me that we are all the same. The words he said out loud are the ones we so-called "normal people" say to ourselves in our head.*

THE HUNT FOR HAPPINESS

Alcohol, food, sex, exercise, and drugs are a few examples of things that provide a fleeting jolt of pleasure, but leave us wanting and needing more.

Happiness is only temporary, so people are always on the hunt for a new adrenaline rush. An American study showed that the happiness subjects felt after getting a new job, new relationship or new apartment wore off after just three months. Today we shop more than ever, but that doesn´t give us long-lasting satisfaction either.

When are we going to learn? Many people are completely convinced that the next relationship, renovation, vacation, child, job, etc. will finally make them truly happy.

> **"Our longing for the future makes us forget to live now."**
>
> **Chuang Tzu**

Many people are so obsessed with the future because they are so dissatisfied with the present. Too many think that money will buy true happiness. Well, let´s do a thought experiment. Let´s say you win the lottery. You´re happy for a few months, then the dissatisfaction creeps back in and you are back to square one. If you don´t practice living in the now, you will never be able to enjoy it.

True joy can only be experienced in the now!

Micael Dahlén, professor at the Stockholm School of Economics, writes about the "Coveting Society" in his book Nextopia:

Now that the internet makes everything so accessible, we think that happiness lies somewhere in the future, not in the present. On TV and on the computer we see all kinds of possibilities and things to be had that make us mad with envy, and make our everyday realities seem gray in comparison.

Many people are restless and long to be somewhere else, in some other time. Their here and now is rarely or never good enough.

Do you find that days, months, and years rush by all too quickly? There is only one way to put the brakes on our experience of time – that is by living more consciously in the present!

Everything and Still Nothing:
Friends of ours with two small children ages four and six spent almost the whole summer travelling, their schedules full of activities and events. They visited amusement parks and friends all over Sweden. When we saw them in the early fall, we asked them how their summer was. They replied: "It feels like we were everywhere this summer, and still nowhere!"

HAPPINESS IN THE BLINK OF AN EYE

When the well-known Swedish footballer Henrik Rydström played the last match of his career, something very special happened:

My last match was over. When I looked up into the stands I saw a very familiar face. Aldor, my childhood coach, had traveled 62 English miles to see the match. I went over to him, reached out, took his hands and said: "Aldor, how nice to see you." He had tears in his eyes and couldn't respond. It was one of those moments, a moment that fastens and stays with you. It makes every tough training session in the wind, cold and snow worth it. Makes it worth everything.

In this magical moment Henrik was truly present to life and got a glimpse of the now in its greatest most beautiful form.

Life's most joyful moments happen when we are the most focused on and present in the now.

To learn to be more present to life is the beginning of a fantastic journey, a journey that leads to more inner peace, sharp awareness, happiness, and vitality than you have probably ever experienced.

Early in your journey, you may only be able to experience short glimpses of the now, but with more training and practice, you will be able to experience it for much longer periods of time. What is much easier to do in the beginning is to take a step back and observe your own thoughts, and state: **There's this endless chatter going on in my head, but I am here listening to this chatter.** When you listen to and become conscious of your thoughts, you not only become more aware of what they are, but you also come to see yourself a witness to your thoughts.

A new consciousness has appeared in you.

Every time you create a break in the otherwise constant stream of thoughts, your contact with the present grows. For most people those openings only happen rarely and coincidentally. They can happen in connection with strong experiences, physical intimacy, or extreme physical exertion. Suddenly there is a priceless stillness. Unfortunately these moments tend to be short-lived, and the stream of endless chatter takes over again.

It has been proven that if we can be emotionally and mentally present to what we do, we will feel intense happiness.

To learn to spend more time in the now is the best gift you can give yourself.

If you want to make a change in your life, choose to focus on being present in the moment as often as you can. Make it a habit to take your attention away from the past and future as much as possible. Try to notice how often you are in the here and now. **This will help you to quickly move to being present in the moment.**

Snap out of your unconsciousness. Use all of your senses. Ask yourself: Who is with me? What sounds do I hear? What do I see in my surroundings? What scents do I smell? Make sure to avoid value-based statements and judgments around what you experience, avoiding words like good and bad. Notice your breathing. Feel the air flowing in and out.

Direct all of your focus on the now and say what problem is going on in this moment.

Your problems will reduce when all of your attention is focused on the NOW!

NOW-EXERCISES

Learning to be more present in the moment requires much practice and patience. One reasonable goal is to try to create more moments of complete presence, and spend less time thinking about the past and the future. Every time you manage to create a break in your stream of thoughts, your connection to the present grows. The challenge is to practice a few of the following exercises regularly:

MEDITATION/BREATHING

Focus on your breathing as often as you can throughout the day. Every moment of focus on your breathing helps. When your thoughts wander away from you, take note and put your focus back on your breathing. Do it for one minute, five minutes, or half an hour!

Close your eyes. At every inhalation, think "I'm breathing in". At every exhalation, think "I'm breathing out."

Focus on your breathing. Breathe and let everything be as it is.

FOCUS

Wherever you are, occasionally take a deep breath and ask yourself: **What is happening here and now?** Pay full attention to whatever you are doing and experiencing in that moment.

AFFIRMATION

By repeating the following affirmation for a minimum of one and a maximum of three minutes at least once a day, you will strengthen your intention to live more in the now:

"I choose to stay completely and fully in the now."

STOP THE STREAM OF THOUGHTS

To experience five to ten seconds of presence in the now, quietly ask yourself:

"I wonder what my next thought will be?"

BODY SCANNING

Work towards increasing your body awareness, so that you pay attention to your whole body. **Look for an app or search on the internet for an appropriate CD.**

YOGA/QIGONG

Combined body and breathing exercises strengthen your physique, make you more conscious and present, and help you improve your body awareness.

QUESTIONS TO ASK YOURSELF: DO YOU LIVE IN THE NOW?

Answer the following questions with either "very often", "rarely", or "never":

- How often do you think that everything would be better if you only did this or that?
- How often do you feel like your life is rushing by outside of your control?
- How often have you been disappointed because your vacation or time off, didn´t accomplish what it needed to?
- How often do you put other people first?
- How often do you feel like you don´t have time to reflect upon everything that´s happening in your life?
- How often do you ignore your physical symptoms without trying to heal them?

If you answered "very often" to four or more of these questions, you should see if there is something you can change with your approach to the now. If you answered "rarely" or "never" to most questions then you have hopefully come a long way already.

Mull over your answers to these questions and think about how they fit in your own definition of happiness.

These questions come from the Swedish book Culture For Health´s Sake by Eva Bojner Horwitz.

THE BILLMARK METHOD

The following method will help you to become more conscious and present in the now.

1. **Say now, aloud or silently to yourself.** This makes you pay attention and creates a break in your stream of thoughts.

2. **Focus on your next five breaths.** Say quietly to yourself, "Breathe in. Breathe out."

3. **Say what you are doing right now, aloud or to yourself. Be detailed and specific. Don't use value-based words such as good, disgusting, ugly, or nice.** Example:
   "I am sitting at the computer and writing an email to my son. Now I am sending it." Or "I am eating a salad that has tomatoes, cucumber, and shrimp. I am taking a bit on my fork and putting it into my mouth."

Try to practice one or all of these exercises at least once a day.

Concentrate on your breathing as often as possible. Focused breathing is the key and the foundation of living a more present life in the NOW!

THE EGO

"Humanity stands before an important choice. We either continue to live in the old EGO-oriented consciousness, or we choose the new PRECENCE-oriented consciousness."

Eckhart Tolle

The ego hates the NOW, and sees it as only a distance to be crossed so that we can become happy sometime in the future.

The ego can never have enough, nothing is good enough.

To achieve what the ego calls "happiness" people hunt for power, money, approval, possessions, and physical strength. For a short while they feel a little better.

As long as your ego drives your life, you will always be on the hunt for new experiences, gadgets and kicks... The ego´s needs are never satisfied. When the ego is in power, you will always experience feelings of inadequacy and fear.

The ego never wants to sit still, constantly seeks approval, and has a strong need to judge other people. The ego also needs constant control and always has sky-high expectations.

The strength of your ego depends on how much you identify with your thoughts and how you let the chatter in your head steer your actions and choices.

We need to see ourselves from the outside and say: **Here I am, and there are the thoughts that whirl around in my head.**

> **"The ego becomes a false identity, where we believe that we are separate, from each other and the rest of the world."**
>
> **Wayne W. Dyer**

The bigger your ego is, the farther away you are from your real, authentic self.

You are not your ego. Your ego is your self-image, your social mask, the role you play.

> ***Facebook:***
> *When I started the Facebook page "Living in the NOW", I got a taste of how powerful the ego can be. From the start the page was a big success. My ego grew in proportion to the number of new likes we received every day. Every time I visited the page I got a*

confirmation that I and the page were well-liked, and I got a huge endorphin kick out of it. My ego felt so good that I started to visit the page as soon as I felt a little down and wanted a new shot of endorphins. I became dependent on getting new likes and positive comments.

Eventually Susan "woke me up" by saying, "Don't you think it's wrong to live through your ego when you write that people should do the exact opposite?" Then and there I woke up and realized how falsely I was behaving. That's how easy it was for my ego to take over, even though I thought I was so conscious.

If you live in the now and feel grateful for everything that exists and everything you are, you will tame the ego.

At the end of the chapter on self-esteem, you will find the Thankfulness Journal exercise. This exercise is also very helpful for minimizing your ego.

Once you learn to live more in the NOW you can say goodbye to your unhealthy ego. In order to achieve inner peace and let go of the hunt for new kicks, we need to get rid of the ego and think less. We will only get there by spending more time in the NOW.

When you identify yourself with the ego, your own value depends on accomplishments outside yourself.

"Apologizing does not always mean that you're wrong and the other person is right. It just means that you value your relationship more than your ego."

Unknown

EXPECTATION ANXIETY

Expectation anxiety happens when we imagine that something disappointing or horrible will happen. The truth is that reality is never as bad as we imagine.

Take note every time you worry that something terrible will happen and later, compare it to what actually happened. You will see that your fears are fantasies that have nothing to do with reality.

Be honest with yourself about how often you react this way. Do you let anxieties take over and keep you from living your life? Do you give up your dreams because all those "what-if" thoughts fill you with anxiety? **How many exciting experiences have you missed because of this?**

> ***Mats said no thank you to a trip:***
> *I was once invited to spend the weekend in Paris, courtesy of my employer. They had worked everything out with the budget; this was going to be the perfect reward for all our hard work. However, at that time I was suffering from intense fear and anxiety, and the*

idea of sitting on an airplane was just out of the question. As soon as I received the offer the negative thoughts started pouring out: What if the plane crashes and I die? What if I have to share room with someone I don't know well and I can't sleep? What if I get lost in a big city and get beaten and robbed? What if I have a panic attack and can't get to a hospital?

I really wanted to go to Paris because I had never been there before. But because of all of these negative thoughts I refused the offer. Once they got back, when my colleagues talked about all the fun they had had, I only felt worse.

Susan made a mountain out of a molehill:
I also experienced letting my anxious imagination get the best of me. We had just moved into the neighborhood. One day I accidentally bumped my door into our neighbor's car in the parking lot. For one and a half days I conjured up horrible scenes in my head about how the neighbor would react. I thought that I had left a mark or maybe even a dent in his car, and I was deathly afraid that he would be furious and yell at me.

Later I saw him in the parking lot and told him what had happened. He told me he hadn't even noticed. There was no dent, there was just a little bit of paint that could easily be rubbed off. He thanked me for my honesty and that was that. I had been worried for one and half days imagining all the terrible things that would happen, and it was all completely unnecessary - what a waste of energy!

These are classic examples of the ability we have to imagine the worst, especially those of us who already suffer from anxiety. Our anxiety wells up inside us and we imagine a lot of negative "what if" thoughts, which gets our adrenaline going. When adrenaline stores in our body we become worried and anxious.

Both negative and positive "what if"-thoughts are an expression of expectation. One fills us with worry and anxiety and the other fills us up with pleasure. **You can choose which kind of feelings you want to create.**

It's easy to continue with the negative thinking patterns mentioned above, but it's not very useful. What is useful is to practice thinking in a positive way. It's all about changing your habits.

Practice repeating the opposite "what if" thoughts that are both positive and realistic.

"Always begin by expecting good things to happen."

Nido Qubein

STRESS – A DISEASE OF THE PEOPLE

Swedish author and journalist Anita Goldman wrote the following a few years ago:

> *We´re not even talking about "warning signals" anymore. We are talking about an epidemic. We are talking about a civilization in deep crisis. We have created a society where we don´t feel well. Not the children in daycare, not the lonely residents of nursing homes, and not our society´s primary symbol of our tremendous progress: the highly educated, highly paid young women who combine motherhood and careers. They don´t combine, they collapse. Can we fix it all by making moderate changes to the workplace, making more positions part-time, and improving childcare? I think the crisis is too deep for these solutions. I don´t think we fit in the society that we ourselves have built!*

Damaging stress is a general disease that can strike anyone. It doesn´t matter if you are poor or rich, young or old, woman or man, employed or unemployed.

We live in the constant buzz of electronics and machines; we very seldom get to experience silence. Electricity has brought with it, the ability to choose when we will be awake. We have considerably lengthened our waking hours, wich has resulted in less rest and relaxation.

Our ancestors woke up with the sun and went to bed when they couldn´t see anymore. We don´t want to suggest that everything was better in the past, but we can actually learn a lot from the past, including many basic skills that have been lost on the road to industrial development. Many of these basic skills are natural extensions of our biology. Our bodies still function the same way that our ancestors´ did.

Our behaviors have changed, but our brains haven´t!

Anita Goldman continues with something else worth considering:

> *(…) Our brains are not designed to deal with the information overload that they are subjected to. (…) instead we are designed for life on the Savannah, where we can work out our feelings in peace and quiet.*

Chronic stress can push many of the body´s systems off balance. Biologically, our body gives clear signals that something is wrong. But our intellect often ignores these signals.

THE DEFINITION OF STRESS

Stress is preparation for extreme physical exertion. Adrenaline and cortisol, often referred to as ”fight or flight” hormones, are secreted in large doses. The ”fight or flight”instinct has been part of our human nature for as long as humans have existed, and the instinct tells us to either run away or fight.

STRESS LEVEL 1

Adrenaline levels, blood pressure, and blood sugar rise – we prepare for fight or flight. The body´s ”rest and digest” hormone – oxytocin – still functions normally. We can easily return to a state of relaxation once the threat is gone. Our body reaches into its surplus energy stores to release as much energy as it can, leading us to feel tense and stressed. We need to physically exert ourselves in order to get rid of the excess energy. Stress spurs us into action. We feel stimulated and enjoy completing the physically demanding task.

STRESS LEVEL 2

Cortisol levels rise and adrenaline levels shoot through the roof. Cortisol causes our bodies fat reserves to break down as well as our muscle proteins. We can store abdominal fat while we consume muscle proteins. Once cortisol levels rise to a certain point our serotonin levels decrease, which leads to depression and anxiety. High cortisol levels and the body´s energy is devoted to physical survival. Oxytocin, the relaxation hormone, decreases. The sex hormones also decrease which lowers our sex drive.

We are often blind to the connection between our physical problems, such as ulcers, headaches, and difficulty sleeping, and our stress level. We don´t see the body´s warning signals and feelings of worthlessness and powerlessness arrive. This can lead to irritability and we can come easily into conflict with those around us. We feel anxious and insecure, without knowing why.

STRESS LEVEL 3

Our stress hormones have been active for so long that we feel like we could collapse at any moment. Our adrenal glands can´t manage to keep up the cortisol production, and they stop working as they should. This causes problems with our mood, sleep patterns, and memory. We are at risk of a serious illness. The body´s production of sex hormones, oxytocin, and other anti-stress hormones is repressed. We show signs of burn out, our work and home lives feel meaningless, and we feel anxious about the future. At this point, we may isolate ourselves from our friends and family. We lose contact with ourselves. At this stage we have too many obligations and find it difficult to listen to others. We may even have memory lapses. We may be plagued by anxiety. We can lose confidence in ourselves and stop caring about what was once important to us. We are stricken with a complete breakdown.

ADRENAL BURNOUT

Adrenal burnout refers to a condition in which due to chronic stress, the adrenal glands stop functioning normally, leading to several different physical and psychological symptoms. Common symptoms include extreme fatigue that is not helped by rest, memory disturbances, nervousness and anxiety, sleep problems, and heart palpitations. The thing is, adrenal burnout doesn´t just happen all of a sudden. It worsens gradually over a long time, so the symptoms are easy to ignore. Eventually, however, they become impossible to ignore, and we end up seriously ill. The diagnosis of adrenal burnout comes after having several stress symptoms during a period of at least 6 months.

IDENTIFYING STRESS

It is important to identify and pay attention to the sources of stress in your life. Once you do this, you can avoid or at least minimize them.

Obviously, there are some sources of stress that you just can´t change. What you change is how you react to them.

You might react in a way that leads to more stress and anxiety, headaches, difficulty sleeping, high blood pressure, ulcers, back pain, difficulty concentrating, depression, and/or low self-esteem. Let´s call this **"reacting negatively."** Reacting negatively is a choice.

What? Blame myself?

At our lowest point, we almost snapped both as a couple and as individuals. Our bodies gave us plenty of warning signals the whole time, but we ignored them. We were always tired and never felt rested. We were almost always irritated, quarrelled over small things, and couldn't concentrate. Our time was completely eaten up by a constant stream of never-ending projects and obligations, but we were never really able to finish anything. We blamed our situation on anything but ourselves, and never realized that we were actually the cause of our own problems and that we were responsible for our situation.

Here are some wise words from social psychologist Bosse Angelöw of Växjö University:

> *We are trained from childhood to be problem-based. Our education teaches us to be problem solvers with critical thinking skills, always looking for a problem to solve. We concentrate on that which is negative at work e.g. conflicts and problems. We never bring up the positive – we don't even know how to. If we were to think of the things that went well at the end of the day instead of the things that didn't, then we would feel so good there wouldn't be any room for stress. Whether we're thinking about our work, family, or hobbies we need to analyze the good in addition to the bad, and then work*

from there to make things better. This positive mindset will turn your thoughts around, and fill you up with energy and positivity instead of stress.

"Many people stress to make money to be able to afford to relax."

Otto Ludvig

TURNING OFF

There was a story in the paper about a famous Swedish artist on the point of collapse. The headline read: "I almost had a complete breakdown, but now I have learned to turn off". When you are feeling stressed, the most dangerous thing you can do is ignore your body´s warning signals. "Turning off" is often the first step towards completely falling apart.

> ***Susan never listened to the warning signals:***
> *For many years I have had the ability to turn off. Problems piled up on top of each other, but I pushed them down. After a while it became easier to push down larger problems. From a young age I suffered in silence, never feeling like I was good enough, never feeling understood. I had tons of friends and I was never bullied, but still I felt alienated. Looking back, I realize I really needed someone to talk to who would really listen. I had nobody to validate my feelings, nobody to answer my questions. I needed someone to tell me that what I was feeling was normal and okay, that other people*

also felt the same way. But I didn't have that. So I just turned off. I floated along in life's ebb and flow, letting myself be pushed by whatever random currents passed through. I didn't steer my own life.

Fast forward a few years: Mats and I were both at our worst. I was even physically sick, but I just turned off my feelings. Yet who else would take care of our daughter and run our home? Afraid to acknowledge my own health issues, I sat stuck in denial. I couldn't imagine how things would work out if Mats and I both fell apart at the same time, so I scraped by on my last reserves. Of course there were moments when I felt like I was going to snap: I would become overwhelmed by panic and feel completely powerless. I carried tension in my whole body, and had chronic back pain and muscle aches. I shrugged it off, determined to plow on with life. I stopped sleeping. I was in a downward spiral, falling into a deep depression. My body was screaming at me to just stop, take a break, breathe, but how could I? I had to push on, just like my father taught me. Relaxation could happen in another life. I had stopped listening to my body and forgot how it even felt to be well. I just thought this was how life was supposed to be.

Mats feared psychologists:
At my worst, what I needed most was someone to talk to. But just like Susan, I had already turned off. I no longer prioritized my own recovery. Instead I focused on the immense stress I felt surrounding our financial situation and the success of our company. My calendar was full of meetings every day; I was everywhere at once. As soon as I checked one item off my to-do list, another took its place. My work was never done, so I never stopped. It became more and more difficult for me to prioritize tasks, think clearly, set clear boundaries and say no. Just like Susan, I felt completely powerless. I slept poorly, developed stomach ulcers, had acute back pain, and suffered from severe anxiety.

I felt like I couldn't go on, but I didn't see a way to get help. I found the idea of talking to a psychologist out of the question, telling myself that only severely mentally ill people needed psychologists.

At the gym I heard someone mention Stig Sjöde, a well-known Swedish mental coach. He sounded pretty harmless and potentially helpful. I contacted him, and soon enough we were talking about issues I had in my childhood. I told him things that I had never told anyone before. Finally sharing these burdens felt incredibly liberating. He taught me some exercises to help me relax, and I began to feel less stressed. Eventually he got me to understand that my own attitude towards myself and my life was the foundation of my problems. Stig also eventually persuaded me to talk to a cognitive psychologist.

My relationship with Susan became increasingly strained. During that period we both found it difficult to communicate, and we consistently misunderstood each other. One day Stig invited me and Susan to talk to him and his wife, Eva. It felt so wonderful to have two outsiders mirror and interpret what Susan and I said to each other, in a way that we could both understand. It felt absolutely necessary to discuss our issues with another couple. In retrospect, we realize this had much to do with our gender roles.

We remain convinced that those conversations with Eva and Stig were the main reason that our relationship weathered the storm. We learned how important it is to listen to one another, to give each other space to think, to compromise. We were the only ones who could change ourselves, and that was what we needed for our relationship to work.

YOU´RE NOT ALONE

The nasty thing about the ability to just turn off is that you stop being aware of how unwell you actually are. When you are completely engaged in work, your focus is directed away from yourself. You don´t notice what you put yourself and your loved ones through. When the weekend or a vacation comes, you feel restless. When your brain finally has a chance to pause and reflect, you feel empty, get a stomach ache or headache, feel completely exhausted, or catch a cold. Monday comes and you turn off again. By this point you´ve taught yourself to turn off whenever you need energy for something else. You ignore your aches and pains, repress your problems and focus on your work. The only thing that could stop you is a sickness that sends you straight to bed or to the hospital.

We never hesitate to go to the dentist when we have a toothache, and we don´t feel ashamed when we take our car into the shop for repair. **Yet as soon as we feel mentally unwell, we feel afraid and ashamed to ask for help. Don´t wait until you no longer have a choice – get help now, before it´s too late.** It´s important to talk to your partner but they cannot replace a professional therapist.

There are several factors that can lead to severe stress. Examples include:

- We want to be seen as strong and invulnerable.

- We are raised to be productive.
- We don´t talk about our problems. We think that everyone else gets by on their own just fine, so we should, too.
- We don´t want to be a burden.
- We find it immensely difficult to ask for help.

Imagine for a second that you don't "have" to do anything.

You are not alone.

It is human to ask for help.

You can change your situation.

And there is ALWAYS help to be found!

IT STARTS WHEN WE ARE YOUNG

Often the high demands we place on ourselves start creeping in during our earliest years. As children we didn´t feel loved for who we were, but rather valued for our accomplishments, such as helping with chores or getting good grades. As adults, we overbook our calendars with things to do because we want to satisfy the most important need of all – to be loved, acknowledged, and liked, which we equate with our performance. We have learned that accomplishments will bring us love!

We are good at satisfying our own and our children´s primary external deeds. We make food when we are hungry, go to sleep when we are tired, and go to the doctor when we are sick. Our inner needs, such as being seen, being validated, getting attention and being happy about something – those are often the ones we forget about.

CHILDREN GROW UP SO FAST

Suddenly a gangly teenager stands before you and presents his girlfriend, and you wonder where mommy´s little boy went. Instead of scurrying around trying to do things for him, be with him.

The most important thing to your children is not what you have, but who you are.

For a person to feel like they are good enough, they need to hear that they are fantastic and special when they least expect it, regardless of their achievements.

Children and adults need to frequently hear:

- I love you!
- I am proud of you!
- I´m listening.
- This is your responsibility.
- You´ve got what it takes.
- I forgive you!
- I´m sorry!

We want our children to learn love, responsibility and to feel happiness. The best way to teach them is to be good role models ourselves.

We need to be the kind of person that we want our children to become!

REFUSING TO GROW UP

Today many young people refuse to grow up. Why would they want to when we make life as an adult look so miserable? We are tired, have financial issues, are always busy and have too many responsibilities.

Do we ever talk about how wonderful it is to be an adult, to feel the freedom that comes with making your own decisions?

We adults need to think about the messages we are sending our children about adulthood. **We are responsible for their interest in growing up and becoming adults.**

It is important for us to be totally honest with our children, and to share our feelings and opinions. We need to show them that we trust them and that they can trust us. We need to talk about the things that bring us joy or weigh us down. Children can understand more than adults give them credit for, and they´d rather understand their surroundings than feel suspended in uncertainty. Children offer important perspectives, and often come up with solutions that we adults don´t see. We should not put too much responsibility on them, but we can give them the option to share their perspectives.

> **"It is easier to build strong children than to repair broken men."**
> **Frederick Douglass**

We cannot shelter our children from life. Life is wonderful, magical, joyful and surprising. Life is also painful, miserable, disappointing and tearful. We need to find the balance in our own lives. In order to feel true happiness, we have to learn what sadness is.

Parents are their children´s teachers, but parents are also people with their own problems, strengths and weaknesses.

Try to forgive your parents if they made mistakes, and accept your childhood for what it was. No healthy person intentionally hurts their children.

ACCEPT YOUR UPBRINGING

People who suffer from anxiety often share certain qualities in their background and upbringing.

Here are some examples of things that you CAN´T change:

- Parents with unrealistic expectations.
- A lack of praise, approval and encouragement.
- Divorce or death in the family.
- Tension in the family.
- Alcoholism in the family.
- Children who take parental responsibility for other siblings or their parents.
- An oppressive emotional environment.
- Family members who don´t express or show their feelings.
- Family members who overreact.
- The feeling that you always have to prove your worth.
- An unstable home life with many unexplained conflicts.

Susan's story:
I remember when I was 12 or 13, I was at my boyfriend's house and I came home one hour past my curfew. When I got home, I saw my father waiting in the doorway. He was so angry about me being one hour late, he practically had steam coming out of his ears. He screamed and scolded, never once asking why I was late. I felt exposed, misunderstood, unloved and alone. I don't remember if my mother said anything during the whole ordeal. She was probably too afraid to come into conflict with my father herself. As punishment I was grounded for a week!

This was just one of many little occurrences that influenced the way I felt about my father for the rest of my life. He always reacted with anger and aggression when he was worried and afraid. If instead he had shared his worries and fears with me, we would have understood each other better. But he never told me how he felt, and my parents seldom, if ever, asked me how I felt.

"Either you run from your past or you learn from it!"

Anonymous

The special characteristic traits of your personality are often caused by what you have experienced as a child.

Her are some examples of things that are completely possible to change:

- Low self-esteem
- Perfectionism
- Nervousness
- Blaming yourself for everything
- Unrealistic expectations
- Anxiety surrounding decision making
- Obsessive thoughts

You can also change yourself if you are:

- Sensitive to criticism
- Overly critical
- Easily affected by other people´s problems
- Constantly concerned with what others think of you
- Constantly worried that you have a serious illness
- Afraid of tomorrow, always asking yourself, "What if this or that terrible thing happens?"

> **"Give your parents just as much forgiveness as you want your own children to give you."**
> **Gunilla Haglundh**

Our whole lives, other people have told us who we are. Has it ever occurred to you that maybe you´re not really your true self?

Accept responsibility for your own life!

Maybe you don´t like the identity that other people have assigned you. Cast it aside and say:

"I want to discover who I want to be!"

Deciding who you want to be – and getting there – will be the most fun and important challenge of your life.

> **"An abused child doesn´t stop loving their parents. They stop loving themselves."**
>
> **Jesper Juul, family therapist**

CHILD AND YOUTH STRESS

We adults are the ones who cause our children stress, and we are the only ones who can help them manage it.

Peter Währborg, professsor and stress researcher, warned us 11 years ago about the impact all this stress has on such young children. He wrote in the Swedish newspaper Aftonbladet:

> *In ten years this generation is going to see an explosion of illness. Atherosclerosis, type II diabetes, and obesity will occur in many young adults.*

Unfortunately, he was right, and that´s where we are today. When he made these predictions we weren´t half as technologically plugged in as we are now. Where will we be in another ten years?

WE WANT THE BEST FOR OUR CHILDREN

As parents, we care about our children´s development. We want to stimulate their growth as much as possible.

Children often go to over-populated preschools and schools. We sign them up for many activities e.g. dance troupes, sports teams, violin lessons and pottery classes. Many parents don´t really know what is happening to their children every day after saying good-bye.

In all these activities and classes, children learn to set high demands on themselves. They also meet teachers and peers with all their spoken and unspoken expectations and demands. Often the unspoken ones are the worst, and the most difficult to manage.

Children meet things daily that stress them – so-called stressors. We can´t shield them from stress completely, but we can talk about it, prevent it, and teach them how to deal with it. We need to be good role models for dealing with stress.

Children need help to identify stress.

Children are more vulnerable to stress than adults, since their brains are in such a key stage of development. Their bodies are also sensitive, and their stress can lead to physical or psychological illness just like it does in adults.

Stress is a reaction to too many physical, emotional, and intellectual demands.

> **"Many parents are ready to do anything for their children – except let them be themselves!"**
>
> **Banksy**

CAUSES OF YOUTH STRESS

Every child is unique and will react to tough situations in their own way. Here we list some examples of situations that, especially in combination, often lead to stress in children and teens:

- Too high demands placed on youth: being asked to learn things that they are not physically or psychologically mature enough for.
- The death of a loved one.
- Parents separating or remarrying.
- Parents who work or travel a lot.
- Unemployed parents.
- Not being understood or not understanding.
- Getting a new sibling or siblings moving out.
- Fighting between family members.
- Never getting to be alone with an adult.
- Never getting time to themselves, or not having a space where they can be alone.
- Difficulty at school, threats of violence at school, bullying, and conflicts with teachers.
- Too many relationships, too large pre-school or school classes, too many substitute teachers.
- Moving to another town or city.
- Not having a voice in decisions that impact the whole family.

- Being away from parents, for example going to summer camp or a school trip.
- Too many activities (overstimulation) or too few (understimulation).
- Getting or losing a pet.
- Puberty.
- A loud environment.
- Too much TV, cell-phone, or computer usage.

One or two of these stress factors are not usually physically or psychologically damaging.

However, children today are often exposed to many of these factors all at once.

We adults should pay extra attention to what´s going on in our children´s lives and how they are feeling.

ACTIVITIES AT THE EXPENCE OF REST AND REFLECTION

Our society tells us that if we´re not doing something all the time, we are lazy and unproductive. This can affect our attitude about taking breaks and generally relaxing.

It´s not uncommon for children in pre-school to have two or more extracurricular activities outside of daycare each week! Many children are not given the time to reflect and work through what they have experienced during the day. To do this they need peace and quiet. When will we teach our children that peace and quiet are just as important as activities?

It is during rest and reflection that curiosity is stimulated. It is during that time that they begin to think for themselves and become individuals. Unfortunately many children today are always so engaged in one structured activity or another, they don´t know what to do with themselves when they have a bit of down time. Peace and quiet make these children restless, even afraid.

Often we adults can´t stand the whining and nagging that occur when children don´t have something to do. We put on a film or sit them in front of some computer game just to get some peace and quiet. If the child has time to reflect they will, in time, be able to create their own activity. This process leads to their development.

We adults just need to give it a little time.

> ***Our Elsa:***
> *Our temporary foster-child Elsa spends every other weekend with us. She shows up at our door on Friday afternoon extremely wound up and hyperactive. She wants something to happen as soon as she steps through the door! Friday afternoon is a calm, quiet time for our family to unwind from the week and make dinner together. If we leave her alone, she either*

chooses to help in the kitchen or goes to her room and work on something. Sometimes it can take her until Sunday evening to really wind down.

When we adults are stressed, we have a hard time seeing that our children are also stressed!

INDICATORS OF CHILD AND TEEN STRESS

Below is a list of some common signs of stress among children and teens. If you notice several of these behaviors at once or in a short period of time, your child may be suffering from severe stress:

- Changed temperament – more introverted, touchy or aggressive.
- Difficulty sleeping, nightmares.
- Restlessness and difficulty concentrating.
- Frequent trips to the bathroom.
- Never or always wanting to be alone.
- Exaggerated amounts of computer, TV, or cell phone usage.
- Head- or stomach-aches.
- Thoughtlessness, for example losing track of time.
- Skipping school.
- Using drugs.
- Perfectionism.
- Teeth grinding, stuttering.
- Physical violence towards themselves, others, or animals.

- Verbal abuse and degradation of others, bullying.
- Breaking things.
- Loss of appetite.
- Putting their fingers in their ears in hectic situations to escape.
- Biting cheeks, lips, and fingers hard enough to leave wounds.

Children and teens can also have physical reactions to psychological stress, also known as psychosomatic symptoms. These can include:

- Stomach pain, vomiting, diarrhea, or constipation.
- Eczema.
- Tension headaches or aches in the neck, back, and shoulders.
- Asthma.
- Sores and other open wounds in the gums.
- Tics.

A BIG RESPONSIBILITY

When we get a puppy, we go to dog training classes and do everything we can to learn how to take care of the dog in the best possible way.

When we become pregnant we read everything we can about how babies grow in the womb, and how to take care of the baby before and after she is born. If only we could hold on to this curiosity during all of a child´s development, even through the teenage years, and continue to learn more about what they need at all ages.

> ***Active parenting:***
> *There are many opportunities to improve your parenting skills, for example through parenting books and courses. We were once invited to such a parenting course ourselves and are so thankful that we got to participate. It was a class in Active parenting, and we highly recommend it. We came away with a better understanding of the kind of parents we were, as well as plenty of advice, and tips about how we could change what we wanted to change.*
>
> *Still, sometimes the immense responsibility that we had for our daughter Julia scared us. We wanted her to grow up to be an independent, empathetic, free-spirited person who lives life to the fullest.*

Many adults feel unwell nowadays for all kinds of reasons. Children sense that something is wrong, and feel like they must be somehow to blame. If you are a parent and you feel unwell, it´s a good idea to talk to your children about it. Children should never have to feel it is their fault. Children can be surprisingly wise and understanding. Not knowing what is wrong is a burden that can weigh heavily upon them.

We have an obligation to ourselves to feel well and live the best lives we can. When we do this we will have a much easier time seeing and understanding what our children need.

Never blame a child for how you feel!

A Child

A child who is criticized learns to judge,
A child who is beaten learns to fight,
A child who is mocked learns to be shy,
A child exposed to irony feels guilty.

BUT

A child who gets encouragement learns confidence,
A child who is met with tolerance learns patience,
A child who is praised learns to appreciate,
A child who experiences fairness learns justice,
A child who feels friendship learns to be kind,
A child who feels safe learns to trust,
A child who is liked and hugged learns to feel love in the world.

From the Swedish book Life Without Borders by Annastina Vrethammar

HOW TO PREVENT CHILD AND YOUTH STRESS

At this point you´re probably wondering how to shield your child from as much stress as possible. Well, stress is contagious, so the first thing you can do is try to feel as well as you can yourself. It may sound selfish, but if you are at peace with yourself it is easier for you to really see your child, to listen and be sensitive and present to their needs. Your child does as you do, not as you say. If you stress about things, so will your child.

SPEND A LOT OF TIME WITH YOUR CHILD

If you have multiple children make sure that you get to spend time with each one alone. If you are two parents, it is important that each parent spends time alone with each child. Spend time together doing nothing else than being together – let it be silent sometimes.

PHYSICAL AFFECTION IS IMPORTANT

Being touched makes children feel relaxed and secure. When we are touched or massaged, our body releases the rest-and-digest hormone oxytocin. Oxytocin lowers our pulse and blood pressure, which in turn improves digestion, increases pain tolerance, and strengthens the immune system. However, if your child does not want to be touched, it is important to respect their wishes. If your child refuses to be touched, you may feel slighted at first, but you should feel proud of your child´s ability to set boundaries and verbalize their needs.

LISTEN TO YOUR CHILD

Many children and teens have big problems with not having any adults to talk to. They may not have an adult near them that they trust enough. Sometimes children just need to talk to someone who will listen.

TALK TO YOUR CHILD ABOUT WHAT YOU FEEL AND THINK

Talk to your child about all sorts of feelings: pleasant, frustrating, angry, loving, whatever. This will strengthen the bond between you. If you let yourself be vulnerable, sincere, and honest with your child, they will learn to treat you the same way. Accept and validate all of your child´s feelings. Let them be sad, angry, or disappointed. Try not to smooth over their feelings because they make you feel uncomfortable.

LOOK FOR AGE APPROPRIATE ACTIVITIES

There is a lot of literature out there about child development. Take the time to learn about your child´s development so that you can make well-informed decisions about what activities they participate in. It is not always easy to know what is good for your child. We do not instantly become child development experts as soon as we have children, but we can make an effort to understand. You can talk to your child´s pediatrician if you need recommendations for books or other resources. Also, remember that what the child wants is not always what they need.

LET YOUR CHILD BE BORED SOMETIMES

Try to weather the nagging and whining when nothing

is happening or when they don´t know what to do at the moment. It is good for children to have free time to do nothing. It is out of "nothing" that creativity and imagination flourish. Sooner or later the children will come up with their own game or activity.

PAY ATTENTION

Spend some time every day studying your child´s behavior. Try to get a picture of your child´s rhythms and how they react to different situations, so that you know when something is suddenly off.

CREATE ROUTINES

Children love and find comfort in the familiar. Repetition makes them feel safe. Sometimes parents worry that children will be bored by repetitive activities and routines because they themselves are. Children love fun routines and traditions that bring the family together. Once the child reaches puberty they may want to break away from them but these family traditions will return as fond memories of their childhood when they get older.

HELP YOUR CHILD TO SET BOUNDARIES

Children often have a hard time setting limits for themselves, especially when it comes to TV, cell phones, computer usage, bed-time, or how many toys they should have. Even if they protest the limits you set for them, they need them and will benefit from them.

According to Teija Nuutinen, researcher at People´s Health Research Center in Helsingfors, Finland, school aged children should not have more than two hours of screen time per day.

> ***Julia needed help saying no:***
> *When our daughter Julia was six years old, she had some playmates who lived very close by. She would have played with them 24 hours a day if we allowed her to. We noticed that she needed help saying no to her friends. We sometimes told them that Julia had to spend some time with us at home. She occasionally protested, but after a while she always enjoyed herself just spending time with us. We wouldn't do anything fancy, just talk, listen to music, or play a game together. She sometimes told us later that she didn't even really wanted to play with her friends.*

CHILDREN AND ANXIETY

If you are a parent with anxiety issues, it is important to watch out for signs of anxiety in your children because anxiety can be inherited.

Here are some common examples of anxiety symptoms in children:

When children show an exaggerated fear of

- abandonment,
- serious illness,

- criticism,
- making mistakes and embarrassing themselves,
- not fitting in or
- germs.

Children's anxiety can sometimes also manifest as

- difficulty concentrating,
- hyperactivity,
- excessive nervousness or
- a lack of self confidence.

Many children can show mild versions of these behaviors without necessarily suffering from anxiety. It is only very exaggerated forms of these behaviors, and if the child shows many of the behaviors together, that suggest a serious case of anxiety.

If you suspect that your child is suffering from anxiety, contact a doctor who can refer you to a good child psychologist or therapist.

> ***Separation anxiety:***
> *One of our friends has an eight-year-old daughter who suffered from very anxious behavior and separation anxiety. She desperately needed to know where her parents were at all times. The girl's mother couldn't take out the trash without the girl needing to know where she was going. She was always worried about not fitting in and always needed*

to look perfect. Her hair clips always had to be straight and her clothes had to be perfectly ironed. She didn´t believe in her ability to do things she hadn´t done before. Her parents tried to encourage her, but she was so afraid that she did not even try the activities. They sought help from a child therapist and today she is free from these problems.

We hope and wish that you do not feel guilty or feel like a bad parent after reading this. Maybe you may feel that the information in the chapter is depressing to read and that there is a lot to deal with. If that´s what you are feeling, be glad – you have received an insight and can finally begin to take action.

Take one step at a time – you can do it!

"Do something today that your future self will thank you for!"
Anonymous

SELF-ESTEEM

The negative and hypercritical thoughts that torment your self-esteem can start in early childhood. Unfortunate circumstances and events can have led to you feeling rejected, out of place, and like you don´t fit in.

Maybe you were rarely received praise, or were unfairly punished, criticized, or even abused. **You may have come to the conclusion that you were worthless, dumb, no good, or inadequate**.

This leads to, among other things, that you see yourself as worthless and unimportant. You may not dare to say what you think because you are afraid of being rejected or you believe everything has to be perfect. Every time that you do get rejected, or fail at something, or risk losing control the old conclusion that you are worthless, dumb, etc. is activated.

Sooner or later you develop terrible anxiety, and with the anxiety come habits that make it hard to function. You avoid all conflict, are overly careful, are quick to quit, or just don´t dare to do anything at all.

All of this becomes a confirmation that you were "right." You think more self-critical and self-deprecating thoughts, such as: "I´m inadequate," "I´m a bad person," "I´m dumb," "I´m worthless," etc. The vicious cycle continues and can lead to depression.

Many children and adults struggle with low self-esteem. When we don´t believe in our own self-worth, we may seek affirmation from other people or confirmation of our value through material possessions.

> **"It doesn´t always show on the outside how it feels on the inside."**
> **Anonymous**

When we increase our self-esteem, we also increase our acceptance for other people´s faults, and we find it easier to work together. We begin to like ourselves more, we are more satisfied with ourselves, and we don´t criticize ourselves as much.

High self-esteem gives us courage. We dare to take up a little more space in social situations, we dare to say what we think, we dare to make decisions and connect with new people. People with high self-esteem lift other people up, know when to be humble, and make space for other people to be heard.

In order to raise our self-esteem, we need to praise ourselves often for who we are, not just for what we do. When we dare to challenge ourselves to do things that we haven´t done before or that we are afraid of, our self-confidence grows.

In order to raise your self-esteem, you can start by treating yourself and those around you in a new way.

What you think about yourself is much more important than what other people think about you!

When you focus on the positive in your life, you become more optimistic and spread positive energy all around you. You will also get more positive energy in return. It takes practice, but it is possible to become more positive and change the way you think.

Try to surround yourself with people who inspire you, support you, and wish you well.

Surround yourself with positive messages and affirmations.

Write notes to yourself and stick them on your refrigerator, mirror, laptop, or anywhere else you will see them each day.

A good exercise to make a habit:

Write in a Thankfulness Journal every evening.

Keep a notebook by your bed. Every evening before you go to sleep, write down three things you are thankful for. You can write about something from that day, or something from life in general. You can also write down some aspect of yourself or someone else that you appreciate.

WORRY

An 85-year-old man who learned that he would soon die said the following about worry: **"If I could live my life again, I would have more real problems and fewer imaginary ones."**

Research shows that the average Swede worries for about 20 hours per week. It is therefore probable that severely stressed people worry twice as much! Imagine instead using these weekly hours being present in the now or working on positive goals for the future.

Many anxious people are also hypochondriacs. They are constantly worried about getting some incurable illness.

When you worry about the future try the following: ask yourself several times how likely your feared scenario is to occur. Is it realistic to expect it to happen?

Eventually you will notice that almost none of your fears will come true.

Ask yourself out loud: **"Why should I worry about something that hasn´t even happened?"**

Mats Shares His Worry Story:

I often worried that something terrible would happen to Susan or Julia, especially when Susan went on a long trip or plane ride. I immediately conjured up horrifying scenes of plane crashes and highway pile-ups. I even worried about how we would get by after her death. I couldn't concentrate, felt splintered. Became confused and only got more and more anxious.

Now I don't waste my time on speculations. I ask myself if my fears are realistic – hardly! Can I influence Susan's situation with my worrying? Absolutely not!

Sometimes I worry about my health. If my worries seem realistic then I don't hesitate to go to the doctor and ask them to do whatever tests are needed. If the tests show that my thoughts were justified then I thank myself for seeking medical help in time, but I know that the probability that they will find some sickness is very small!

THIS IS HOW YOU GET RID OF UNREALISTIC ANXIETY

Save ten minutes every night to be your "worry time," for example 8:50 to 9:00 pm. When you start to worry about something during the day, stop and tell yourself that you can think about it at 8:50 and no sooner. You will find that once 8:50 rolls around and you are supposed to deal with all your worries, you will have forgotten 90 per cent of them!

For the worries that just won't go away, do something constructive:

- Write down on a piece of paper what is worrying you.
- Write down what measures you will take to eliminate or minimize the problem.
- Write down when you will take those measures.
- Make sure that you carry them through.

Another effective method is called "The river":

Imagine that you are sitting by a stream or river. Large maple leaves fall into the water and float away with the current. Imagine that you lay your worries and anxious thoughts on the leaves and let them sail away.

"Only worry if worrying helps."
Anonymous

ANXIETY

Let´s start this chapter on a positive note.

Anxiety is often a sign of positive traits and abilities. You are probably smarter than average, extremely creative and have an active imagination. These are wonderful qualities! There is research that shows that if you use these unique qualities in the right way you can be the best parents, partners, friends etc.

Unfortunately those of us with anxiety issues tend to use our brain power and creativity to scare ourselves sick. We over-analyze everything and we use our active imagination to create terrible disasters.

When we let our worry and anxiety take over, we question every little thing we do.

Life becomes a constant series of tests and trials instead of an exciting adventure. Many people have gotten so used to their worry and anxiety that they accept it as just a part of life. It is only once you have dealt with your anxiety that you truly realize how much time, strength and energy it has cost you.

Worry and anxiety leads to those creeping feelings of discomfort whenever we find ourselves in stressful or high pressure situations. People who suffer from anxiety often experience:

- Frightening, uncontrollable thoughts
- Depressing feelings
- Severe headaches
- Sweating
- Heart palpitations
- Feelings of helplessness
- Severe fatigue – exhaustion
- Feelings of panic
- Muscle tension
- Feelings of worthlessness

These symptoms of anxiety can also lead us to take on defensive attitudes like aggression or suspicion.

Fear of Death:
Henrik was a man of about 30 who worked as an economist in a large Swedish company. He had been married for four years and had a two-year-old son. Nobody knew that Henrik often worried about death. One day, he suddenly felt a sharp pain in his chest. He was sure he was having a heart attack and went straight to the hospital. The doctors could not find anything wrong with him. This scenario repeated itself a number of times over the next six months. Henrik also began to imagine that he had a

terrible disease. When he felt pain in his back he became deathly afraid and imagined it was cancer. After a few days with a headache he felt panic at the conviction that he had brain tumors. In order to suppress his anxiety Henrik started to drink more and more alcohol. Eventually he realized he needed professional help. Henrik was suffering from anxiety.

Three out of four people in Sweden have experienced psychological illness, either in themselves or in a close relative. It is so common that it affects a majority of Swedes! Psychological illness is the number one reason for sick leave in Sweden. Despite all this, very few people speak openly about their issues. Sadly, the silence can lead to many people waiting too long to ask for help.

WHAT IS ANXIETY?

Anxiety is an emotional disorder, a mental state characterized by strong feelings of fear, worry and nervousness that can derive from a real threat but that usually arises from imaginary threats. **The problem is that our brain cannot tell the difference between real and imaginary threats.** Our body reacts the same way to both, with a full on fight-or-flight response, leading to the release of adrenaline and anxiety when we fantasize about something we believe will happen.

Our worry and anxiety come from our own thoughts, not from other people or the world around us. Problems arise when we dwell on negative thoughts about the past and worries about the future.

We make the mistake of believing all the negative thoughts we imagine.

> ***Mats' anxiety:***
> *I have had terrible anxiety almost my whole life. Since I was seven years old I constantly imagined that terrible things would happen. I always felt like something was wrong. It was first when I turned 25 that I realized that I suffered from anxiety. It was such a relief to finally be able to put a name on all those feelings I had always had. I learned that anxiety was not an incurable illness, but rather something I could control and even get rid of. When I realized how much energy my anxiety stole from me and how it limited my life, I was ready to do the hard work needed to get a handle on my worry and anxiety. – This was the best decision of my life.*

Three important steps to overcome fear and anxiety:

- Learn what mechanisms underlie fear and anxiety.
- Learn effective techniques to change our way of thinking, behavior, emotional responses, and actions.

- Practice our new skills by doing things that previously made us uncomfortable.

CHECKLIST FOR DEALING WITH ANXIETY

- Is it likely that your anxiety-scenarious will occur?
- Try to look at the situation realistically.
- Use facts when you make predictions.
- Use all available information, including positive information.
- Treat your ”what if” thoughts as fantasies, not facts.

Severe anxiety can be difficult to overcome on your own. We recommend that you seek help from a doctor and discuss how you feel about your situation.

If you decide to take medication, complement it with behavioral therapy with a psychologist or a behavioral therapist.

> **“Worry is a waste of time. It changes nothing. The only thing that worry and anxiety does is steal your happiness and take you away from the present.”**
>
> **Mats Billmark**

GUILT

People who feel guilty spend time and energy dwelling on the past.

We may also feel guilty about our everyday lives such as:

- that we should spend more time with our children, partners, friends, or parents.
- that we should eat better and exercise more.

We want to be friendly, kind, helpful, and supportive of everyone, but then we would barely have any time left for ourselves. Suppose we take care of everyone else and put ourselves last. This can lead to feelings of self-contempt and disdain, because we are disappointed in ourselves when we fail to say no or set boundaries. We feel guilty and disheartened; we become angry, irritated, and depressed.

We might also feel guilty about something from our childhood that happened in connection with a broken family, e.g. separations, abuse, or other traumatic experiences.

Whatever happened to you as a child was most likely not your fault. Even so, you have been tormented and carried your feelings of guilt for many years.

> ***One Woman's Story:***
> *One woman who contacted us told us that she felt guilty for years for not loving her parents. She did not have an especially good relationship with them growing up. They never talked about feelings, and nobody ever asked her what she felt or thought. She felt like she just existed - without much purpose or design. She never received encouragement, praise, or support for anything she did. Conflicts were never solved, they were just brushed aside and ignored. She couldn't talk to her parents about her problems. During her whole childhood she felt there was something wrong with her because she couldn't say that she loved her parents. She felt distressed, thinking that she was not normal. As an adult she has reached the insight that there was nothing wrong with feeling the way she did, and that it was not her fault. She has accepted that it was what it was and has forgiven her parents. Their relationship is somewhat better today and she can see them without feeling guilty.*

When you can forgive yourself for things you did and felt in the past, your feelings of guilt will disappear.

You are only human. You sometimes need to think about yourself.

Learn to dare to say no.

Let yourself be lazy sometimes.

Allow yourself to make mistakes.

Learn to set boundaries!

Whatever the cause of your feelings of guilt, they are often combined with low self-esteem. Self-esteem is how you see your worth as a person, how you value yourself.

Work to accept yourself and like yourself for who you are.

In order to let go of guilt and anger, we need to learn to forgive ourselves and others. It's easier said than done, but it is only then that we can leave guilt behind and move forward.

> **"When you forgive, you don't change the past, you change the future."**
>
> **Anonymous**

EXPECTATIONS AND OBLIGATIONS

Are you often disappointed in yourself or those around you? Disappointment goes hand in hand with expectations that are too high. Our unrealistic expectations create constant disappointment in our lives.

This leads to us feeling stressed and worried.

We have all experienced going to a party and finding that it's not at all as fun as we expected. This happens because we have spent so much time building up an idea of how the party would be. On the other hand, many of us have also had an amazing time at a party that we stumbled into by chance. We build up expectations when we are not living in the now, but instead focusing on the future.

If our everyday is grey and bland then of course we focus on all the fun plans we have in the future, but this becomes problematic if we only live for what will happen in the future. However, if we make our everyday a little more special and learn to appreciate the small things, it is easier to focus on the now. Then we have no need to build up expectations around what will happen, and our longing to be anywhere but here and now, decreases.

When you feel depressed about something it can be because something or someone hasn't lived up to our expectations.

Sometimes things go wrong. Plans fall apart. People disappoint you. They won't always be honest, and they won't always treat you like you treat them. They won't always be fair.

But, you can choose how you react, and what attitude you will have when it happens.

Mats' Example:
If I am preparing for a lecture I can choose to stress myself and worry beforehand. I could say to myself: "Mats, you can't mess this up, say the right things and don't forget anything!" I could make myself so nervous that I couldn't even get on the podium. But I can also choose to have realistic expectations for myself and say instead: "I am well-prepared for this lecture. I am going to do the best I can and no matter how it goes I promise myself to be content because I did my best." Do you see the difference? The way I feel going into the lecture is quite different in each case. When I have realistic expectations for myself, I don't feel pressured, I feel relaxed, and the lecture goes much better.

We often set unrealistic expectations for ourselves to look good and feel well - all the time. It's inhuman!

NOBODY looks good all the time and EVERYONE feels bad now and then.

We also want our parents and our partners to be proud of us, but we need to realize that our worth does not depend upon our performance or accomplishments!

Instead of striving for perfection, you should strive to feel as good as you can and be as content with yourself as you can in a world that is neither fair nor perfect.

By lowering our expectations, being more realistic and being more content with what we already have, we can live a more peaceful life.

The more realistic our expectations, the greater the probability that we will be content and feel that we are fine just as we are.

> **"We think too much and feel too little."**
>
> **Charlie Chaplin**

RECOVERY HAPPENS WITH CHANGE

In order to avoid damaging stress and anxiety we need to make changes. We need to change our expectations and our old values. **We need to create a new understanding of ourselves, other people, and the world around us.**

Have you thought of all the things we feel obligated to do in our lives? We constantly place expectations upon ourselves. We try to:

- become better parents,
- become better partners,
- spend more time with our families,
- earn more money,
- go back to school,
- lose weight or
- change jobs.

Where do all these commitments and promises come from? Some could be from your parents, friends, or partner.

Make a list of all the things you "have-to" do. **Remove the ones that aren't your own.** Some of your "have-to"s are realistic and some are not. Do you need to lose weight for your health or to satisfy your partner's nagging?

Do you want to go back to school because you want to, or because your parents always wanted you to "make something of yourself"? **Be honest with yourself.**

What you should do is to change your "have-to" into realistic goals. Make sure they are things that you actually want to do.

Once you have decided which of your "have to"s you want to do and they are your own, not someone else's, you can change them into goals in your life. Think carefully about how you will achieve them. Make a plan so that you can take the first step tomorrow.

Remember that it is never too late!

You are never too old!

It all depends on how much you believe in what you want to do.

There is no failure!

The only way to fail is to not try at all!

> **"When was the last time you did something for the first time?"**
>
> **Anonymous**

WHAT IS PERFECT?

Just as we seek perfection on the outside, so we seek perfection inside. We want to feel inner peace, happiness, and balance.

The problem is that we want, believe in, and strive for a life where everything is perfect and problem-free. But it's not easy being human, and sometimes we make things harder than they have to be!

A more realistic goal is to feel that the length of time we feel at peace, happiness, and balance increases and that these moments occur more frequently. Then the feelings of stress and anxiety will decrease.

Our society tells us that our lives should be perfect, and if they're not we should be dissatisfied. If we have this attitude we will never be happy! We should stop even using the word perfect. Nothing is perfect! Or maybe everything is perfect.

Our perfectionism can keep us from trying to do certain things. We think: "Why even try when it will never be perfect?"

Our society tells us that we should be a certain way, live a certain way, and look a certain way in order to be "good enough". These are "perfect" ideals that many people strive for. Depending on our age, gender, job, and other factors, we can have different ideals that we are expected to strive for.

It hurts to see children who won't dare touch crayon to paper for fear that it won't be "perfect". Already they know what is considered "nice" and what will be liked by the people around them.

It also hurts to see a teenager scrutinize themselves to pieces just because ideals say they should look a certain way. Teenagers try to live up to impossible ideals created by media, other adults and the rest of society.

Adults want it all to be perfect: children, partner, home, and hobbies should all make up a perfect façade to show the world. They invite friends over for dinner and they are sometimes completely exhausted before the party has even started.

No person is perfect - or you could say we are all perfect, in our own way!

> ***Absurd Demands?:***
> *Here is a typical example. A female acquaintance of ours described one time she invited some friends over for dinner. As usual she wanted both the house and the dinner to be perfect. An hour before the guests were to arrive the living room was full of Lego, the children hadn't changed their clothes and the meal was half-finished. Standing over the stove she felt*

her blood pressure rise, sweat ran down her forehead and her heart was pounding. Half an hour later she was lying on the bathroom floor throwing up out of sheer stress and exhaustion.

We live with an illusion of how everything ought to be. Who even wants to grow up with perfect parents and friends? How could someone live up to such an environment? It would lead only to feelings of frustration and a constant feeling of inadequacy. Everything would become a competition.

When we try to live up to all of our own and society's expectations, we feel like we're about to crack. From the outside it looks like we're getting by just fine, but inside a constant conflict rages on. We feel hunted, inadequate, and guilty. Sooner or later it begins to show on our bodies. We shrink up and get quiet. We look down and become worrisome and anxious. We feel stressed and get stomach aches and tension headaches.

"I'M FEELING HORRIBLE, THANKS"

When you ask people you know, "How are you?" you often get the following response: "Oh, everything's fine, how are you?" If they were to truly tell you how they felt then you would probably be standing there for a long time.

We believe that everyone else is doing just great. But everyone has their troubles and maybe we would all feel a little better if we dared to talk about them. We need to have the courage to show each other our weaknesses.

Has it come to the point that we don't have the energy to care about each other in this way? Don't we have the time?

Instead, we try our hardest to make sure other people don't see our problems at home, in our relationships, at work and in ourselves.

People are afraid to show their vulnerability. Who wants to be a whiner? But speaking honestly about your situation is not whining at all. **We need to deal with our problems. A part of dealing with our problems can be to talk to someone about them.**

> ***Some Words on Vulnerability:***
> *People are often asking us how we dare to be so open and personal. People call us brave. They ask us if we don't find it scary, if we aren't worried that our openness is going to bite us in the behind. But it is obvious to us that we should be this way. If you are going to write a book and lecture about this topic, then it is a huge advantage, if you can tell stories about yourself that resonate with people. We have never experienced our openness as something negative. The opposite in fact! It is incredibly unfortunate that more people don't realize this. When we dare to open up and share ourselves and our stories, we get an infinite amount of positive energy back.*

I, Susan, worked for a few years as a high school teacher. I was always very open with my students - I shared a lot about my family, my life, and what I thought about things. From my perspective it seemed like the students really appreciated it when I opened up and showed them who I was. They felt safety and security in my openness.

VULNERABILITY MAKES YOU BEAUTIFUL

Brené Brown, research professor at the University of Houston, is one of the world's leading experts on vulnerability. Her research shows that vulnerability is the core of guilt, shame, and fears of abandonment. At the same time, vulnerability is necessary for making the connections that we humans long for most.

Brown's research shows that people love to see vulnerability in others. When we make ourselves vulnerable we show our authentic selves, we understand each other and we feel kinship and connection. BUT - few people want to show their vulnerability!

Her research also shows, that those who make themselves vulnerable most, readily are also those most willing to let go of who they think they should be, and instead dare to be themselves.

For those people, it was difficult and scary to expose themselves in this way. Yet for them, vulnerability was not a choice, but a need. They believed that what made them vulnerable, made them beautiful! This group of people had many stable, authentic, loving relationships. They were able to get close to people without fears of abandonment or rejection.

THREE MYTHS ABOUT VULNERABILITY

Vulnerability is a weakness. This is the most dangerous myth. Having the courage to make yourself vulnerable is a strength.

You can choose not to be vulnerable. It doesn't work to just not be vulnerable. When we try, we isolate ourselves, and distance ourselves from other people. What we need to do instead is to ask ourselves: How do I react when I am vulnerable?

Vulnerability has an on/off button.
Making yourself vulnerable doesn't mean you have to show all your feelings all the time. Every time you dare to be more open with yourself and others, you become braver. These rewarding moments will encourage you to be more vulnerable and authentic in the future.

> **"One of the most difficult challenges in life is to be yourself in a world that tries to make you just like everyone else."**
>
> **Anonymous**

Some people fear that they are not good enough as they are. They fear what others will say about them if they don't live up to how they "should" be. But the opposite is true. When we show our human side others like us more. Our openness makes it easy for other people to recognize themselves in us and connect with us.

Humans want to recognize themselves in others, we then feel an understanding and empathy for one another. That makes us feel better!

It is fantastic to be able to affect and touch others!
Everybody wants to be affected!

Today we spend so much time and energy on social media showing our lives. The social media have strengthened our belief that everyone else has it better. They have more interesting jobs, more exciting vacations and are happier than I am.

Not many people upload pictures of their botched and burned casserole or the crumbly cake that fell apart in the oven.

Few write on Facebook about the jobs they didn't get or the vacations they couldn't afford. We don't want to be "losers".

What makes us think that life is a competition?

> ***Social Media:***
> *Susan and I have Facebook pages, homepages and blogs. Of course we want to be positive*

and write about things that give energy and inspiration to others. But we have noticed that when we dare to write very personal things like our problems, or discuss things with more depth, we get more comments and likes.

"There comes a point when you realize that you will never be good enough for some people. The question is: Is that your problem or theirs?"

Anonymous

HEALTHY THOUGHTS

The most important steps you can take to end your stress and anxiety are to live more present to the now and talk more positively. Negative thoughts throw us into downward spirals of stress and anxiety. It is so easy to criticize and blame ourselves.

Whether we acknowledge it or not, our brains are always thinking. These thoughts constantly influence our mood and emotions. When we feel worried or stressed, this is usually due to negative and unhealthy thoughts.

Our families and our upbringing have a huge influence on us and the way we think. Did you often hear your parents fight? Did people in your family complain and show dissatisfaction with their lives?

What kind of messages did your family send? How were you influenced by the behavior of the adults around you?

When we grow up surrounded by people who fight, complain, and spread stress, it's hard to develop high self-esteem and self-confidence. **It is, however, completely possible to fix this as an adult.**

We have a hard time admitting that we have negative thinking patterns. We do everything in our power not to admit it. **Once we realize that we have negative thoughts, we can change our behavior and get better at thinking positively.**

The effects of this positive mental shift will exceed all your expectations.

Do you worry often? Do you have self-destructive thoughts? Do you analyze everything? Do you doubt your own abilities? Are you unhappy with how you look?

95 per cent of all of our negative thoughts aren't true! They are made up fantasies. However, the positive, life-affirming, strength-giving thoughts are true!

Our brain can't tell the difference between fantasy thoughts and real thoughts, and always reacts by believing that each thought is real. This can lead to big problems when your thoughts are mostly self-destructive or self-deprecating. On the other hand, thoughts can be very effective tools when we use positive thoughts in the right way.

NEGATIVE THOUGHTS - AN ADDICTION

Negative thoughts are addictive. Once we experience some of the (short-term) benefits of negative thinking, it quickly becomes a habit. **There is a point to being negative,** otherwise we wouldn't continue thinking this way! When we think negatively, we focus on the negative within ourselves, resulting in negative actions and a way of speaking to those around us. It can lead us to getting attention from other people who listen and show us empathy. We use their good natured behaviour to help us and support us when we have problems.

Another benefit of our negative thinking patterns is getting out of things we don't want to do. Since our loved ones feel sorry for us and don't want to overtax us, they either help us with our obligations or lower their demands on us. In this way we use our negative thoughts to avoid doing things that make us uncomfortable or that we just don't feel like doing.

What do you get out of your negative thoughts?

This question may seem strange but it is necessary to ask. Being a negative thinker is like having an addiction, If your life is driven by stress and anxiety, you need to admit that you are a negative thinker. It is only then that you can do something about it! Hard work is needed to break the unhealthy habit. We are creatures of habit so it requires a lot of work to change our way of thinking.

To think negative thoughts all the time is like being abusive to yourself.

> **"The grass isn't greener on the other side, it's greener where you water it."**
> **Anonymous**

HOW CAN YOU RECOGNIZE A NEGATIVE THOUGHT?

Do you think the question is silly? You may believe that you don't have many negative thoughts that disturb you. The following items are "hints" to help you see if you do…

Negative thoughts are thoughts that make you feel weak, unwell, and worrisome. They cause you to feel stressed, angry, depressed, bitter, afraid, anxious and sick. They fill you with guilt and shame. They make you feel lonely, unattractive, insecure and unloved.

If you often feel some or all of these things, your mind may be tuned to negative thinking. If so, you're not alone - most people have hundreds of negative thoughts every day.

People with low self-esteem tend to look to others for approval and affirmation. We want other people to tell us that we are good enough, that we are attractive enough, and that we are special.

Here are some examples of things you can do to change your behavior.

- Be honest with yourself. Realize how your negative thoughts hurt you.
- Try to understand your negative thinking as a bad habit that you need to change.
- Decide to spend all of your waking time and energy breaking your unhealthy thinking patterns.

- Become conscious of how you think.
- Lift yourself up with self-affirmations and encouragement, instead of seeking validation from others.

These examples come from the book From Panic to Power by Lucinda Bassett.

How do we know that we have positive and healthy thoughts?

Positive thinking makes us strong. It makes us feel well, secure, happy, loving, attractive, relaxed, balanced, brave, energetic, motivated, safe, loved, and accepted.

Seeking validation, negative people spread their negativity around. If you feel that you have people in your surroundings that have negative behaviour that drains you, you should instead look for people who behave differently.

Remember, that misery doesn't just love company, it needs it!

Be patient with yourself. Breaking bad habits takes time.Your current negative behaviors have surely taken years to develop. Changing a bad habit is like learning something new.You need time to change your way of thinking. It takes patience and persistence.You need to understand how positive thinking patterns work, and then practice, practice, practice until they become your natural way of thinking.

Be conscious of how you think! It is never too late

to become the person you want to be. Pay attention to what you actually think, and reflect upon your thoughts at the end of each day. It might help to write "Thoughts?" on your hand to remind yourself to stay conscious.

It is only when you become conscious of your thinking patterns that you can change them.

> *We constantly remind, our daughter Julia, that she is good enough just the way she is. That she is a wonderful girl and we are proud of her. It is important for her to hear this often, even when it's not connected to any kind of achievement. It strengthens her as a person in so many ways.*

Praise your child often for his or her wonderful personality, not just for accomplishments.

Imagine if we had all received praise, encouragement, and affirmation during our whole upbringing! We would have been spared so many anxious and worrisome thoughts and benefited from a much better self-esteem.

> ***Mats Thought he was Such a Positive Person:***
> *I refused to accept that I was a negative thinker. It's so easy to believe that we are what we wish we were! Once I became more conscious of my thoughts I realized how wrong I was. I discovered that my negative thinking patterns were making me sick. I would never have*

been able to help other people with their stress, worry and anxiety if I had continued with my own negative thinking. After 30 years I finally decided to put a stop to it! I have learned that you can change as an adult and I am a living example of this. I am a normal person who was completely broken down from stress and anxiety and who felt alone and ashamed to have these problems. Now I have learned that change is necessary to become healthy and that change can only come from within.

Giving yourself healthy, positive praise will bring you a long way towards feeling better. Praise from within strengthens your self-esteem and self-confidence, makes you more motivated, and helps you stay relaxed in stressful situations.

We have a tendency to focus on the negative and shrug off the positive. Try instead to focus on the positive around you. Let your mind linger on times of happiness, joy, and hope, instead of on the negative.

> **"The happiness you feel in your life is determined by the quality of your thoughts."**
>
> **Buddha**

Here are some exercises to help you become more conscious of how many negative thoughts you have:

- Always have something you can write on, either a notepad or cell phone. Whenever you have a negative thought write it down and at the same time write a positive replacement thought next to it.

- Be aware that you substitute every negative thought with a realistic, positive thought that you can actually believe in. Otherwise you are just fooling yourself.

Begin by writing down one negative thought per day. Later, write down one per hour and then one every half hour or more often.

Choosing to think positively and talk positively to yourself, to others and about others makes your life more meaningful!

Pay more attention not only to your thoughts, but to the things other people say. Write down negative comments from your colleagues, children, partner, and friends. You will be shocked by the amount of negative talk that you hear every day.

This is a very effective method.

> ***Some of Susan's Experiences:***
> *I used to work with teens aged 15-19. It was painful to see so many young people with low self-esteem and little self-confidence. Many did not like themselves. Occasionally they forgot to be self-conscious and were just present in the moment and not caring about their*

surroundings. These were the times when they dared to show their beautiful, intelligent, fun, unique personalities. Otherwise they were so afraid to be themselves, embarrass themselves and not be "good enough". It was so absurd! I think there are too few adults to guide them through all the pressures they face. We adults need to be better role models. We need to show our whole selves, to dare to be different in a genuine and honest way. We need to be courageous enough to show when we make mistakes, be sad and willing to take a stand on a topic.

Children are born with a total tolerance for differences, but somehow this disappears by adolesence. Many young people are not tolerant of differences in each other. What happens? Where does this tolerance go? Do they learn to judge and ridicule others from us adults? I often think back to when I was younger, how I sought affirmation from everyone but myself. What others thought of me was very important. I had low self-esteem and never dared to try new things. I constantly sought confirmation that I was good enough, especially from boyfriends. I often did what they wanted, including spending all my time with them and ignoring my own friends. Later in life I sought praise from my employers. Whether from bosses or boyfriends, I thought I could improve my self-esteem by being good enough for someone else. Nobody ever told me that I was good enough just as I was!

Mats' Experiences:
Growing up, I suffered from the worst worry and anxiety: my well-being was dependent upon hearing from others that I was good enough. I had an enormous need to be affirmed, to look good, to say the right thing and to be a good brother, son, and friend.

Now Susan and I have gotten much better at lifting ourselves, each other and others. Saying kind things to yourself is an important skill, and it is not shameful or egocentric. This skill helps us to grow as people. It strengthens our self-esteem and self-confidence. We feel better and dare to do what we want, and we enjoy it without feeling guilty!

It is incredibly liberating to stop caring what other people think or say about you. So stop looking outside yourself for praise. **Give it to yourself.**

> **"Neurotics use other people's eyes to look at themselves; healthy people use their own eyes to look at the world."**
>
> **Fritz Perls**

Leave stress and anxiety behind. You can do it. You are unique, special, and full of potential!

Once you have learned to change the way you think, life will be full of new possibilities. Everything is possible, and there is no such thing as failure.

> **"I don't have everything, but I love everything I have."**
>
> **Anonymous**

You have surely noticed how easy it is to be dragged down by someone who is miserable, frustrated, and angry. It's just as easy to be lifted up by someone who is happy, excited, and optimistic.

Your new positive behavior will not only bring joy to you, but to many people around you as well.

This chapter is so important. Please feel free to re-read it many times.

> **"If you always think how you have always thought, you will always do as you have always done.**
>
> **If you always do as you have always done, you will always get what you've always gotten."**
>
> **If you want your life to be different you have got to think differently!**

YOU ARE WHAT YOU THINK

Our Friend Linda Shares Her Story:
On Monday, September 9, 2013 at 8:40 a.m. our whole life collapsed around us. Like a bomb, like a punch in the face, like an unexpected lightning strike, my husband and I got the news: I had breast cancer. It was most likely a large tumor. My whole right breast would be removed on Thursday. I remember collapsing on the floor. I had had no idea I was sick. Not even a suspicion. Nothing. The opposite in fact: I was happier, stronger, and healthier than ever. Or so I believed. Now I thought, I am going to die. This is the end. I will never survive this. I don't want to die. My children need their mother.

Since the operation was to happen so soon after we got word of the tumor, my husband and I didn't have time to let the news sink in, didn't have time to find the "right way" to tell our children who were 4, 10, and 12 years old. We were forced to tell them that same night. And so we did. When I uttered those words to the children, that I had breast cancer and was going to have surgery, I realized I had two choices: Either I could completely fall apart, lie down, pull the covers over my head and give up. Or I could do a mental suit of armor, sharpen my sword, climb up on my warhorse, and ride into battle - to win! - like Jonathan Lionheart. I went with the second option.

I wouldn't have made it through such a terrible ordeal otherwise. I had to make an active choice. I chose to win. The insight that I had in that moment, saved my life. I'm not saying I didn't fall apart, cry, scream, throw dishes, lose my breath in panic or that I have no fear of death. It is about finding the inner strategies to use when the worst thoughts come. I was operating on a foundational belief that I would win. Happiness and life would win. Chemotherapy and radiation put me through the ringer, but I just saw it as part of the battle. It was just something I had to go through in order to win. I sharpened my sword often so that it would always be sharp. Cancer is a dragon, a monster - and it will be slayed!

We can always choose how we want to think in every situation, so that we are able to handle the situation in a better way.

People who see problems everywhere often create problems around themselves. People who instead see opportunities, create opportunities! It sounds like a cliché but it's true.

Take some time to observe how the people around you are.

Which people around you always see problems? Which ones see solutions and possibilities? Which ones are the most pleasant to work with and spend time with? What kind of person do you want to be?

You create yourself through your thoughts.

Every thought that you have about yourself or someone else creates either peace or some form of discomfort.

A person who is willing to learn and develop, and who accepts herself despite her flaws, radiates a calm energy that is contagious to others and inspires respect.

Your thoughts influence how you feel, act, and react. Everything you say and do depends on how you think. You have the power to choose how you think - don't let anyone else make that choice for you.

Taking control of your thoughts is not always so easy, however, because it also requires you to take full responsibility for how you think, act, and react.

It's all a question of attitude: to your own life, to other people's lives, and to the connections between you!

A MORE MEANINGFUL LIFE

Instead of always hunting after more, you can train yourself to fully appreciate what you already have.

Your loved ones are the most meaningful things you have! Find someone to love and nurture your relationships. Communicate, encourage, and listen.

Be present to the moment! Look around you: the most meaningful things in life are free. How does your partner or child look when they sleep? How many colors are there in your garden? When you are truly present in the moment, you will notice more and more of these little things and you will see how much energy and strength they bring you. Learn to enjoy the little things. **Remember what a treasure a totally ordinary day is!**

Be generous! Humility goes a long way. Despite all your problems, you are probably more privileged than many others. Maybe you can be a good role model for someone close to you.

Learn to appreciate your life! Learn to live, not just exist!

> **"The less you care about negative people the more peaceful and beautiful your own life will be."**
> **Anonymous**

DISCOVER NEW SIDES OF YOURSELF

What would you most like to do in your spare time?

What are your strengths?

What are you especially good at?

Who do you want to spend time with?

Where would you most like to live?

Young people have dreams. Why do so many of us stop dreaming as we grow older?

What did you dream about when you were younger?

Have any of your dreams come true?

What do you dream about now?

What would it take for you to fulfill your dreams?

Write down your dreams.
You may find that they are not impossible to achieve, and only you know what is best for you!

Do it now! For your own sake!

> **"What we are today comes from our thoughts of yesterday, and our present thoughts build our life of tomorrow: Our life is the creation of our mind."**
>
> **Buddha**

IRRITATION AND ANGER

Going about our daily lives we seem to be pleasant, happy, upbeat people. Things at work might annoy, anger, or frustrate us, but we don't express these feelings. Instead we just let them rot and fester inside us. We keep a smile on our faces and hide our true feelings.

When we come home, and the mask comes off and we relax, it can be our family who bears the brunt of our unmasked anger. The irritation and anger we bear is often expressed at home.

Those small things that annoy us every day build up over time, and eventually they turn into anger.

It is truly unfair and tragic and those we love most become the trashcans for our aggression, anger, and frustration, while people we barely know get to see the nice and positive side of us!

Did you grow up in a family where people used their anger and stubbornness as a method to dominate and control? If so, it's possible that you have also learned to use anger to get your way. You may not be conscious that you're acting this way and that you're hurting yourself and others. Try to break the cycle before you pass it on to your children. If you don't, you risk your children remembering you as the parent who always came home angry and irritated.

> ***Mats Shares:***
> *My good friend Lasse recently told me a story about when he was 15 and his father worked as a salesman for a bread company. His father often visited supermarkets in the area Lasse grew up in. One day Lasse went to a friend's house after school and started talking to his friend's mother. She worked at the cold cuts counter at one of the supermarkets that Lasse's father visited. When she met Lasse she asked him: "Isn't your father the one who works as a salesman for the bread company?" Lasse nodded, wondering why she wanted to know. "Your father is the nicest and funniest salesmen who visits us!" Lasse was very surprised to hear this since his experience of his father was the exact opposite. Lasse's impression of his father was a sour and angry man who came home from work, ate his dinner in silence, and then fell asleep on the sofa 20 minutes later with the newspaper over his face.*

This is a classic example of when strangers get the nice, good side of a person while family feel the negative consequences of a tired and exhausted person.

People who suffer from stress and anxiety are often

irritated and easily become angry. If you are someone who uses your anger to control others, you come off as an unpleasant person who is insecure and lacks self-control.

A person with high self-esteem doesn't need to show their strength through aggression and anger.

Reflect and ask yourself, have you ever benefited from your anger? Is it worth exposing your body to the stress response that comes along with the anger, including high blood pressure, increased pulse and sweating? Anger brings on the same adrenaline rush as anxiety and the feeling after is the same. Do you achieve what you want through anger? What are the consequences? What fears are you hiding with your anger? How do you feel afterward? What consequences does it have for the relationships between you and the people you direct your anger towards?

> ***We Kept up Appearances:***
> *Several years ago, Mats and I worked together in our shop. Even at our most stressed we kept up appearances outside our home. Nobody could have guessed how we felt inside. We gave good service, smiled at our customers, and we were pleasant and friendly to them. We hid any annoyance we felt in our interactions with them. Yet we often didn't have the energy to be so pleasant to each other as we were to our customers!*

When we came home from work we collapsed. We struggled to get the most basic things to work in our home and in our family. We quarrelled often and became irritated with our daughter Julia. We could sometimes overreact to small things.

Susan had a short fuse and I found it uncomfortable to be around her when she got so upset. She could get really angry over nothing. I tended to withdraw whenever she got angry, and that made her even more angry. Once things had cooled down, neither of us wanted or dared to talk about what had just happened. We never solved our conflicts and our anger just festered.

I, Susan, thought Mats was afraid of confrontation since he never wanted to discuss anything. I didn't understand that it didn't work to have a discussion with me when I got so angry. I had learned how to win in an argument by being so angry that the other person just gave up!

CONTROL YOUR ANGER

There are ways to turn the negative anger into something positive and more effective.

When we are tired and irritated, we react automatically with anger without thinking about it.

Try to think before you react.
Blowing up at people is a bad habit that we have learned through repetition. You need to learn a new way of dealing with your stress and frustration. Once you feel the anger rising within you:

Take a step back to avoid a spontaneous reaction, otherwise you will act the same way you always do.

Pause for a few seconds, take a few deep breaths and reflect on the situation.

You have every right to be angry, but do it in a well thought out way! Be decisive and make sure you keep a calm voice. Staying calm works better; people will listen to you and respect you in a completely different way.

Avoid making accusations, such as "You were wrong!" or "This is your fault!" When you do this, the other person becomes defensive and will not listen to one more word of what you have to say. When you scold or yell at people they feel attacked and they shut down immediately. They become completely occupied with thinking about what they will say to defend themselves and retaliate.

If you feel like you have to criticize someone, always start by saying something positive. If you want to criticize a colleague, start by saying something like, "You are a very hard worker and I really enjoy working with you. However..." Then take up the issue at hand. Talk about how you experience the situation without raising your voice, say: "I feel that..."

Always use I-statements, as opposed to you-statements, when describing how you feel and what you experience. Say, for example: "I feel sad about..." or "I really need to talk about something that happened..."

Choose your words carefully, maintain a normal voice volume, and stop before you repeat yourself. Tell the other person that you appreciate that they are taking the time to listen to you. This will put a positive end to the conversation. That person will then be more willing to have similar conversations with you in the future.

WHEN SOMEONE TURNS THEIR ANGER ON YOU

Do you take it personally when someone else directs their anger at you? Don't! It doesn't necessarily have to do with you. Often a person has a lot of other unrelated conflicts and they just direct all their frustration at you, or they are too tired and stressed to deal with the situation in a better way.

People may try to make you angry or get a rise out of you or get you off balance but how you decide to react to the provocation is up to you. It's your choice!

When you are dealing with angry people, take a step back. Ask yourself: "Why are they so angry? What's behind the anger?" Then tell yourself: "I don't need to take this personally. This doesn't necessarily have to do with me."

"People don't lose their tempers, they use them."

Rudolf Dreikurs

LET GO OF ANGER

Strive to let go of old anger. Don't dwell on the past. This will only make you bitter and depressed. It only hurts yourself and you will find it harder to focus and be present in the moment.

When you come home to your family feeling angry and irritated about something that happened during the day, **tell them what happened, and tell them that your anger and irritation has nothing to do with them!** That simple action and way of communicating can spare you many unnecessary episodes of irritation, misunderstanding, and guilt.

REMEMBER that you are a very important role model for your children! Children do what we do. Do you want your children to handle their anger in a positive way? If they learn that anger helps you get what you want, they will use that method. Anger is an important feeling to express, but you can choose to express it in a constructive and controlled way instead of an aggressive and uncontrolled way that leads to more problems and misunderstandings.

Break your old bad habits and both you and those around you will feel much better. People will also be more willing to listen to you.

COMMUNICATION

Poor communication is the largest cause of relationships failing. We assume that we understand each other when we actually don't, and these misunderstandings lead to pain, anxiety, and more misunderstandings.

If you communicate clearly and don't take things for granted, your relationships will work much better.

We often think we speak more clearly than we actually do. This can be because we all have different ways of expressing ourselves. Something that sounds totally clear to you can still be unclear to someone else. A third person might find it overly clear and even patronizing! The most important thing is that your message gets across. Ask the other person if they understand, and if they have any questions.

If there is something you don't understand - ask questions! Don't be content until you are sure you understand the message. By daring to ask questions you show that you are interested and eager to understand. You can start by saying: "Just to see if I understand correctly, do you mean that...?"

Verbal communication is made up of two parts: speaking and listening.

Being an open, clear, and concrete communicator is just as important when listening as it is when speaking. Let everyone involved speak for themselves and be heard.

Be direct, clear, and concrete. Tell exactly what you have heard, seen or witnessed, how it influenced you and how you feel about it. Clearly state what is important to you and share your feelings. Tell the other people involved that you also want to know what they think and feel. This shows that you care and are willing to listen.

It is especially important to think about how we communicate with our children and how our communication styles will influence them. If we adults often complain about how we look, so will our children. If we gossip and spread rumors about our neighbours, work colleagues, family and friends then so will our children!

Ask yourself if you are communicating something to your children that you'd rather not. This applies to both verbal and behavioral communication.

What can you do to change this?

> **"Sometimes it seems like it's more important what other people think of us than what we think of ourselves!"**
>
> **Susan Billmark**

Stop Caring:

I, Susan, have noticed that the older I become, the less I care about what other people think. This isn't the case for everyone, but for many people this comes with maturity. What is important to me in life has changed. When I was in my 20's and lower 30's I thought it was important to iron my sheets, clean the house once a week, do my grocery shopping on Fridays and always eat breakfast. I did all this because this was what my mother had done, since it was just how it was supposed to be done. I don't mean to say that my mother was wrong, I just mean that we do things by habit, without ever asking ourselves if we want them to be this way.

Nowadays I don't care if it's a little dusty, and I don't iron my sheets. I know I don't have to feel guilty if I don't eat breakfast and I don't do the week's shopping on Fridays because I buy too many things that we don't need and we end up throwing them away. I often wonder how my life would have looked if I had the same confidence and self-esteem when I was 15 that I have today. Would I have chosen a different profession? Would I have lived in another country? How would I have felt? Would I ever have sunk into a such a deep exhaustion depression?

When we understand why people react in negative ways and say negative things, we don't need to care about it or to take it personally. We can't be hurt by the things they say or do.

It is incredibly freeing to learn not to take other people's negativity and aggression personally. If you make it a habit not to care what other people think about you, you will avoid a lot of stressful thoughts and occurrences in life.

Take nothing for granted and don't take things personally.

> **"Every person I meet has something to teach me."**
>
> **Dalai Lama**

Which statement fits you: Many people are ungrateful and unfriendly or: Nearly everyone is friendly and helpful?

Things we think about others will often be true about ourselves.

DARE TO SAY NO

Not daring to stand for what you do and what you believe in is a common cause of anxiety. You may not speak up even though you would like to.

Maybe you think you do stand up for yourself just because you sometimes get your way. But how does this happen?

Was it through controlled and constructive behavior or through anger?

Anger is no way to stand up for what you believe in.

Aggressive behavior is distinguished by hostility, nastiness, and anger. It leads people to see you as insecure and out of control and it can push people away.

When you express yourself in a calm and honest way, you come across as confident, deliberate, and in full control of the situation. You grow as a person when you learn to describe your needs, say no, and state your intentions. You will also get the respect you deserve.

Are you a people-pleaser who avoids all confrontation? If you fold at the slightest sign of conflict, people will take advantage of you and this will hurt your self-esteem.

To learn to stand for what you believe in, saying no, and staying calm is something you just have to practice until it becomes a habit and happens naturally.

> **"Nobody can hurt me without my permission."**
>
> **Mahatma Gandhi**

There are many reasons why people don't get what they want in life:

- We don't want people to think we are petty or fussy.

- We don't want to be irritating. We want people to like us.
- We don't dare ask for what we want because we are afraid to hear "no".
- We avoid asking for help because we don't want to seem weak.
- We have a hard time speaking up for ourselves when we feel insulted and hurt.
- We want to please others and hesitate to ask for things because it could lead to conflict.
- We don't want to expose ourselves to the discomfort and anxiety that follows conflicts.

Many people are afraid of seeming selfish or hostile if they stand up for what's important to them, but this can be avoided if they go about things the right way.

Speak seriously and decisively without sounding angry. Don't excuse yourself. Use short sentences and stay on the subject. Say what you have to say as concisely as possible, and then be quiet.

Don't come up with a lot of excuses, for example that you don't have time, aren't interested etc. You will then risk the other person trying to talk you into it. Just say: "Unfortunately I can't today" and then talk about something else or end the conversation.

Susan Shares a Friend's Story:
My friend worries constantly. I believe this is because she can't say no or stand up for what she wants. By now her daughter has learned that her mother will fold as soon as conflict arises, and exploits this to get what she wants. My friend's behavior stems from the fact that she is afraid that her daughter won't like her or think that she is a good mother. But in reality her daughter is losing respect for her. What her daughter needs is a mother who can stand up for her beliefs and principles in a calm and deliberate way. Such a mother becomes a good role model and someone to look up to.

I remember one time when my friend and I made reservations at one of our city's best restaurants. We were both looking forward to having some time to ourselves to eat good food and catch up. We had just gotten our dinner when my friend's telephone rang. It was her 17-year-old daughter complaining of a stomach ache and asking her mother to come home. My friend gulped down her food and rushed home to take care of her daughter.

Just like that our evening was over. My friend was afraid of the conflict that would have arisen if she had said no to her daughter. She later told me that her daughter's stomach-ache was just her way to get her mother home to make her dinner. My friend felt terrible because she had been manipulated by her daughter. She also felt guilty because she had left me in the middle of our dinner date.

"I dare to choose the important things in life."

Anonymous

To be clear about your intentions and say no when you need to, helps you build up your self-esteem and feel secure in yourself.

Present your opinions in a controlled, nuanced, and thoughtful way!

Don't make yourself feel guilty. Cut yourself some slack, do things because you want to, and stand your ground when there is something you think is important.

Don't wait for other people to make decisions for you. Do it yourself - **you can do it!**

If you want someone to help you with something, you must learn to ask for it. Do it in a deliberate and friendly way with a calm voice and you will most likely get the help you need. The alternative is to not ask for help and then wish you had. Or, you do everything yourself until you snap and then yell at the people around you for not helping. The other people will yell back in defense and everyone will feel like losers.

A person who stands up for and expresses themselves has a strong self-esteem and likes themselves.

We are all role models for each other.
Who do you look up to? Who looks up to you?

> **"They may forget what you said, but they will never forget how you made them feel."**
>
> **Carl W. Buechner**

HAPPY RELATIONSHIP HAVE NOTHING TO DO WITH LUCK

A good relationship is not something you just fall into. Even with good chemistry the best of intentions, the strongest relationships only develop when both partners take the time to care for each other every day. Love is something you have to devote yourself to consciously and regularly.

Many couples spend years looking for the perfect recipe for a happy relationship. It's really quite simple:

- **Give the other person your full attention!**
  In order to have a functioning relationship you need to be fully present. Show your partner respect by focusing on him or her when you are together and not being distracted by a lot of other things.

- **Touch each other often!**
People have different beliefs regarding the importance of sex in a relationship. We know, however, with certainty that closeness and touching each other in a loving way is very important. What you do exactly doesn't matter, the important thing is that you do it. When we touch each other physically we strengthen our bond on a deeper emotional level.
- **Continue to be generous!**
Continue to be attentive to and care for each other the way you did in the beginning of your relationship.
- **Show appreciation for your partner on a regular basis!**
Remember to tell you partner how much he or she means to you. Say that you are thankful for having him or her in your life. Thank each other often.
- **Touch base with each other just because…**
Busy couples can fall in the trap of only talking about practical topics. Who can take the child to the doctor? Do we need anything from the store? Who will make dinner tonight? Happy couples call or text each other just because.
- **Flirt with each other!**
No matter how long you have been together, continue to give compliments,

notice a new haircut, appreciate a new outfit, or just smile flirtatiously at each other.

- **Work on something together.**

A common project strengthens your relationships. A happy couple knows how to work as a team.

- **Have fun!**

Don't take life so seriously. Couples who laugh together have a better chance at maintaining a strong relationship.

- **Be apologetic!**

Remember to apologize. Sulking and pouting poisons everyone around you. Apologizing helps us to grow as people.

- **Support your partner's hopes and dreams!**

Care about your partner's dreams, hopes, and plans. This is love!

One recent study showed that couples who stay together year after year are the ones that show the most generosity and kindness to one another.

> **"It is not a lack of love, but a lack of friendship, that makes unhappy marriages."**
>
> **Friedrich Nietzsche**

AFFIRMATIONS

Affirmations are used for personal development. It is done to, among other things, clarify to yourself what you want to achieve and to be able to more easily reach your goals.

You can also use affirmations to make yourself braver and happier, break a bad a habit, and much more.

The idea behind affirmations is that we create the world around us and inside us through our thoughts, feelings, and beliefs, and this means we hold great power over our lives.

We often tend to think **negative** affirmations about ourselves, for example "I have an ugly nose" or "I'm not good at anything" etc. We all know how horrible we feel when we think like this. The more we have these thoughts, the stronger they become, and the more we let the negative thoughts steer our lives.

If this works in a negative way, it also works in a positive way!

We can use positive affirmations to achieve more positive feelings and more easily achieve our goals.

When you create your affirmations, keep the following tips in mind:

- They should be short. Example: "I am confident."
- They should be positive. Avoid using words like "not", "never", "must", or "should."
- They should focus on the I form and be personal in nature. Example: "I, Susan, am calm and level-headed."
- They should be formulated in the present as if they had already happened. Examples: "I have…", "I am…", "I can…".

Create your affirmations and repeat them regularly and as often as you can. Think them to yourself or say them aloud. Write them down on a paper and put the paper somewhere you will see it often to remind yourself.

Shared Affirmation:
Since we decided to try to help as many people as possible to avoid falling into the same stress anxiety situation that we did, it has been our mission to share what we have learned through this book. We have an affirmation that we repeat to each other and to ourselves to help us in our mission. It goes like this: Learn to Live has sold 500,000 copies and has been published in ten countries.

The point of affirmations is not to trick yourself. It's to change the way you think.

It's to steer you to what you want and to have a more positive attitude to life.

Here are some more examples:

I listen to my heart.

I like challenges and develop from them.

I feel strong.

I eat healthy food.

I am good enough just the way I am.

I am enough.

My body is OK.

My needs are important.

My financial situation gets better every day.

I've got what it takes.

I have everything I need.

I have happiness in my life.

I have all the time I need.

I feel relaxed.

I am brave.

GOSSIP

Have you ever realized the immense power that words have? How much influence we have as soon as we say something to someone? This is especially true with our children. As parents we have an enormous responsibility for how we speak to and around our children and what kinds of messages we send them. They imitate everything we say and our opinions imprint themselves upon them.

Words spoken to us can change our belief about something or someone for the better or the worse.

Why are we so quick to join in when we hear gossip?

> **Fear?**
> *Our theory is we feel less alone when we hear that other people have problems just like we do. We may also find it easier to talk about other people than about ourselves, because then we don't need to take responsibility or share our own issues. It would be much more honest and constructive if we just talked about ourselves instead of other people!*

When you hear gossip about people it stays with you and limits you when you later meet them. You will feel uncomfortable when you are with the person who was the subject of the gossip.

We make ourselves sick when we listen to gossip and talk about people in a negative way. It feels uncomfortable in our entire body. If you instead talk about people positively, you will feel the complete opposite. Give it a try and you'll see a huge difference in how you feel afterward!

Through Other People´s Eyes:
I, Susan, had a student who interned at an office where she didn't get along with her supervisor. Every time I saw her she would tell me about the conflicts between them. I pictured the supervisor as someone who exploited her employees and didn't listen to her colleagues. I had the impression that she was hard, insensitive, and unreasonable.

A few years later Mats and I started to have more contact with that company as more students started having internships there. We got to know this student's supervisor. It turned out that she was kind, positive, and hardworking. She was just trying to achieve her goals. Every time we visited she was happy and service oriented. The problem was that I had started my relationship with her unwillingly, seeing her through the eyes of my student.

We probably miss out on a lot of nice relationships just because someone planted negative gossip in our minds.

Children hear adults spread rumours, judgements, and prejudices about other people, sometimes people they have never met. Children then learn that this is a natural way to communicate.

Imagine a ten year old girl who hears from a classmate that she's ugly. Maybe the classmate says it because he is jealous, frustrated, or disappointed about something in his own life. The word "ugly" sticks to the ten-year old girl, and from that moment she starts to believe it's true. Eventually these types of occurrences can grow in proportion and can lead to anorexia, bulimia, anxiety, and obsessive or self-harming behavior.

We must get our children to understand that what other people say about them doesn't always have to do with them.

> **Mats Shares:**
> *Oprah Winfrey had a beautiful 35-year-old woman on her show, who told the following story about when she was in high school: She was standing by her locker. Suddenly she heard two boys talking about her on the other side of her locker door. They said, "If someone wants to have sex with Jane they'll have to tie a bag over her head first!" And then they laughed. This one sentence completely changed Jane's life. From that day on she decided that she was*

ugly and disgusting. During her entire adult life she never came close to having a loving relationship with someone, instead she was living alone in the belief that she was too ugly and repulsive for anyone to love. One sentence had completely brainwashed her, and repeating it to herself over the years had made it true to her.

It is so important what we say to and about each other!

Exercise:
Decide to not say anything negative about anyone for an entire day. Use that day to listen to what people around you say about each other. You will be surprised by how much gossip is spread.

Become conscious of your words! Use them carefully so that they don't hurt you or the people around you.

Think about the fact that every time someone comes to you with gossip it plants, most often, an untruth within you. Gossip is hard to avoid, but you can defend yourself by saying: "I don't want to hear gossip". Or you can question the gossip, asking: "How do you know this?" or "Is that really true?"

> **"Gossip dies when it hits a wise person's ears."**
>
> **Anonymous**

SCHEDULING AND ORGANIZATION

Do you let time control you or do you control your time?

We are constantly coming up with new technology to help us save time. Yet it seems that the more of these devices we have, the less time we have and the more stressed we are. Of course we can use cell phones and computers to save time if we use them the right way, but we can also become stressed from being so plugged in all the time.

If you don't plan, you will always end up running out of time except for the most important things, which leads to stress. Planning gives you the security of knowing that you will have time to do what has to be done. Then you don't have to stress out beforehand about what you have left to do.

> **"Nothing is impossible. The impossible just takes a little bit longer."**
>
> **Winston Churchill**

Susan's Effectiveness:
One day when I was giving the kitchen a

major deep clean, I went to grab a rag from the laundry room. When I got there I saw that there was wet laundry in the machine that needed to be hung up, but first I had to take the dry laundry off the line and hang it up in the closet. In the bedroom I noticed that the flowers were in desperate need of water. I went into the bathroom to get some water, but quickly forgot why I was there. I went back down to the kitchen and I realized I still needed a rag. I thought I was so effective since I was always doing something, but truth be told things took me much longer than they needed to. I was never paying full attention to what I was doing. I did lots of little things but few big things, and I never felt like I really finished anything. I believe the term multi-tasking is out-of-date. To multitask is very seldom effective. Nowadays it is thought that we should handle things one at a time. I find it most effective and realistic when we completely focus on one thing at a time. Do it well, get it done, and move on. I think this saves a lot of time!

"I DON´T HAVE TIME TO RELAX"

Something that can give you more time is to watch less TV and use your cell phone and your computer less. Think about how many hours a week you sit in front of a screen. How many of those hours could be spent doing something that you'd rather be doing?

According to one Swedish TV report a few years ago, Swedes spend about six hours a day consuming TV, radio, Internet, and newspapers. I'm pretty sure this number has not gone down since.

All the information that we take in during a day has to be worked through and processed at some point in those 24 hours. **We need to plan time for reflection, relaxation, and recovery.**

We can't just cram our brains full of facts, stories, and opinions without pruning some of them away. Every once in a while we need to get rid of things and make space in our heads. We can't do this all in our sleep. In our sleep we have no control over how our brain sorts through our thoughts. That is why it is so important to do conscious meditation and conscious relaxation! It is very important to find time for meditation in our daily lives, figure out how to do this in the best manner, and put it in our schedules. It is at least as important to plan relaxation and meditation as it is to plan physical exercise.

> **TV, Technology and Us:**
> *When our daughter Julia was little, we often turned the TV on for some children's program and then just left it on all evening. Eventually we showed her how she could turn it on by herself, but it rarely occurred to her to turn on the TV while she was playing with something. Nowadays we avoid turning the TV on as*

much as possible because once it's on, it's hard to turn off! The problem today is that digital entertainment is just so accessible. It's so easy to just have the TV on as you scroll through your cell phone or computer! It's difficult to limit our technology usage in a family where everyone wants different things. The most important thing is to talk about how you will deal with it consciously as a family. Disconnect from technology now and then. You can take a walk, talk to each other, or play a board game instead.

EVERYONE CAN HELP OUT

Some children are so catered-to you would think they live in a hotel! **If the whole family helps out with chores there will be more free time for everyone and they can spend more time together.**

Children can be great helpers from a very early age. Each family member putting their own dinner plate in the sink should be a given from a very early age. Small children love to help out if you encourage them from the beginning.

Older children can of course help out with more advanced things. They tend to be very understanding if you explain to them why their help is needed and what the consequences are if they don't help. They learn that a family is a team where everyone needs to work together.

Martin, our Little Helper:

Martin, our five year old temporary foster child, spends a few hours with us each week. With a bit of encouragement, he loves to help out! He seems to treat the chores like a game. He loves to stand on a stool and stir the pot, chop vegetables, set the table, and pour things. He can even dress himself just fine if he knows what he is going to wear. He is probably so helpful and competent because his mother has encouraged him since he was a toddler. We find children at this age to be very willing to help out if adults have a positive and playful energy when they ask them. If adults ask for help in a way that doesn't sound like nagging or commanding, children will often join right in.

Children need to take part in everyday chores and duties in order to feel like they belong and that the home is also theirs. With every task and chore they accomplish, their self-confidence grows. Discuss and share decision-making with the entire family. Children will learn that their opinions matter. They are respected and in turn they will show respect back to you.

Mats′ Spoiled Self:

I am a great example of what can happen when a child doesn't help out with chores. As the youngest of three I was always taken care of. I have a very considerate mother, a handy father, a responsible older brother and a helpful big sister. All of them always wanted to be helpful and meant well, taking care of me out of love and kindness. But the result of all this help was that I was totally unprepared to live alone and had no idea how to take care of myself. My first girlfriend was also in for a real shock. She had moved in with a 26-year-old who didn't know how to do laundry or cook food.

TIPS FOR BETTER PLANNING AND ORGANIZATION

- Write down a schedule.
- Make long-term plans over a month, six months, or a year. Who will do what?
- Make detailed plans over short periods of time, like a week. Who will do what?
- Don't overbook your days. Leave room for things to take longer than planned, and leave space for spontaneity.
- Learn to say no to other people's demands on your time.
- Delegate tasks as much as possible.
- Make plans together as a family.

Figure out which part of the day you have the most energy, and use that time to do the things that are most important and take the most energy. Try to give yourself at least ten minutes every evening to relax.

By even using one or two of these tips you will be surprised how much better you will feel. Improving your planning and organization takes practice, since you need to change the way you see WHAT you do, WHEN you do it and HOW you do it.

You might start to feel guilty in the beginning. Don't. **You deserve to feel well!**

Mats was Fully Booked:
My calendar used to be completely full. I was always rushing: I walked quickly, ate quickly, and drove quickly. I always had so much to do. I set unrealistic goals, never had enough time for anything, and always had to choose between important things. What I didn't get done one day I would push over to the next, and then that day would become even more stressful. Susan had the same problem.

Both Susan and I had a hard time dealing with people who did things slowly or even at a normal pace. We hated standing in lines and got frustrated at people who spoke slowly. We were impatient and found it difficult to relax. I could feel so stressed that I could barely focus on my own daughter when we played together. The whole time I was with her I couldn't stop thinking about all the things I had forgotten to do or needed to do.

One time on my way to my parents I was sitting in traffic feeling stressed almost to my breaking point, even though I had no appointment and wasn't late for anything. I never questioned why I was stressed, it was just my default way of being.

If you recognize yourself in this description then you need to realize the seriousness of your situation. Living this way is not healthy and you need to do something about it now. You need to identify and pay attention to the factors that cause you stress in your life. You also need to change the way you relate to things you can't change.

Make time for yourself and mark it in your schedule. Spend less time on your cell phone, computer, and TV. You need time to regain your strength. Take a bath, close the door to your room, listen to music or guided relaxation, meditate, practice yoga or Qigong, or take a walk, even if only for 15 minutes.

Recovery is priority number one, especially if the life you are leading requires you to maintain a high level of activity.

> **"Last night I made a thousand plans that I promptly forgot this morning."**
>
> **Anonymous**

ORDER

The way our surroundings look is important to our well-being. Messiness and disorder can cause us stress.

In a family, everyone has a different definition of messiness. It is important to talk about our different definitions together, and compromise to reach a common level. In common spaces we need to have common understanding.

Being a perfectionist is not the same as wanting order and cleanliness. Perfectionism is an unhealthy behavior that can lead to obsessions and phobias.

Order is when things are in their correct places. Your home doesn't need to look like a home decor magazine; it should look lived-in.

When we are stressed it can be like chaos in our brains. With all that chaos on the inside, it's even more important to have order around us in our surroundings.

> **We Influence our Children:**
> *I, Susan, used to throw my clothes all over the place in our home which led to Julia doing the same. I understood that I was teaching Julia it was okay. Today she is a teenager and she still throws her clothes everywhere, like many teenagers do. I, on the other hand, have stopped. If I take care of my things, I'm establishing the norm she will grow up with and carry on to adulthood. What we do and*

show our children and youths will eventually "set" as a rule or norm, even though we may find it is hard to believe when they time after time do not do what we do or say!

How are we influenced by clutter?
Do a little test with a room, e.g. your bedroom. Look at your room with an unmade bed. How does it feel? Then make your bed, straighten out the blankets, and clean up your bedside table. Put away all unnecessary items. Stand in the doorway and ask yourself, how does it feel now?

What is the first thing you see when you wake up?
Is that what you want to see? How your room looks can influence how you sleep. What's the first thing you see in the entryway when you come home? Can you improve something to make your home more welcoming - for your own sake?

"Instead of thinking of what you don't have, think of what you do have."

Mahatma Gandhi

TIPS ON HOW TO GET ORDER IN YOUR HOME

NOT TOO MANY THINGS.

Put away or get rid of all unnecessary things that are out, even the things that are under the bed, under the sofa, or are behind a door. Even if you can't see them, you are still conscious that those things are there and it will keep you from feeling peaceful and calm.

CLEAN UP YOUR CLOSET.

When you open your closet door everything should be well arranged. Get a sensible storage system. Have a system for how you stack, hang, lay, or place things.

SOME ORGANIZATION ON THE WALLS.

Paintings, pictures, shelves, and everything you hang on the walls should have contact with each other, the furniture and other items near it. Otherwise, it will feel like they are floating freely on the wall and have a life of their own.

REDECORATING SHOULD BE FUN.

Take one room at a time, study it, move furniture around and see how it feels afterwards. Sort and throw out and let the change take time. Talk together as a family about how you want the room to be. Everyone should enjoy the new space! There are always good solutions to be found through compromise.

EXERCISE

Not too long ago, people led very physically demanding lives that helped them to work off their stress hormones naturally. Today many people have jobs that require them to sit all day, and for these people exercise is especially important.

Physical exercise is incredibly beneficial for people who suffer from stress and anxiety.

It is extremely important for you to get rid of the excess stress hormones you have accumulated during the day.

Physical exercise helps you to cleanse your body of toxins. It improves memory and overall brain function, including your ability to learn and concentrate. Exercise strengthens your immune system, probably by your sleeping better. It is beneficial as long as you don't overdo it - too much strenuous exercise actually weakens your immune system.

It doesn't matter what kind of exercise you participate in. The most important thing is that you do it regularly. **A brisk 30 minute walk every day is an example of good exercise.**

Endorphins, a hormone your body produces when you exercise, make you feel more alert and increase your control over your feelings and reactions.

Exercise helps your body to break down stress hormones as soon as you start working out. You learn how your body works and gain better awareness of it. You feel physically and psychologically more in balance, and you will be more at peace with yourself.

Mats Nedeed to Exercise:
For me exercise has a huge influence over the way I feel. When I exercise regularly I have a much easier time dealing with stress and anxiety. I am happier, have more energy, and become more patient. I know how hard it is to get started, but once you find the right motivation you won't want to stop.

When I exercise regularly, it becomes a habit that I always find time for. I feel pride that I am taking good care of myself and I strengthen my self-esteem and self-confidence.

Make healthy choices, and make sure you find time to exercise regularly.

"The best exercise is the one that is done!"

Anonymous

SLEEP

According to professor Torbjörn Åkerstedt, one of Sweden's foremost sleep researchers, the knowledge regarding sleep's importance over our health has increased. With good sleeping habits, we can lower the risk for a whole host of illnesses, Åkerstedt emphasizes that sleep is vital for our emotional balance. The more you read up on the science of sleep, the more you understand why a lack of sleep makes us more emotional and that it is easier to have mood swings. Underslept, we can overreact to things that don't normally bother us. The latest research also shows that too little or disrupted sleep can lead to increased cholesterol, heart disease, diabetes, depression and exhaustion syndrome. **We need our sleep to repair and rebuild our bodies and recover from the day's damage.**

With too little or interrupted sleep our body loses its ability to rebuild and recover fully. This lack of recovery explains the connection between sleep disorders and stress.

One common cause of sleep problems among people is that we have difficulty turning off our thoughts.

Sleeping disorders are more common in women than men because the disorders are more commonly found in people who work in caring professions such as teaching and nursing. These professions have a high majority of women.

Another cause behind our lack of recovery time is our 24 hour society. We are expected to be available 24 hours a day. If we want to we can be active and entertained around the clock and the line between work time and free time barely exists anymore. Activity late at night disturbs our biological rhythms and leads to shallow and interrupted sleep. Late-night habits lead to poor quality sleep which leads to a poor attitude and decreases our ability to concentrate, which makes us less effective in everything we do.

Most people need about 7 hours of sleep each night to avoid feeling tired and lower their risks for long-term illness.

Susan Ignored her Tiredness:
I have a great need of time alone and find it easy to turn off the need for sleep. As a parent of a small child I prioritized my family and forgot about myself. I started using the night time to study, sew, read, and take care of the house. In the short term it worked out great - I took care of my family during the day and did things for myself at night. But after a while my whole body started to ache.

Today I understand how important sleep is. I know how many issues sleep deprivation leads to for me. Now I pay attention to my body and I recognize the signs it gives me when I'm not getting enough sleep.

Try not to obsess about your sleep problems, however, because this can actually stop you from falling asleep.

When you sleep well, you decrease the symptoms of depression, e.g. worry and anxiety, and you improve your self-esteem.

Focus on the hours of sleep you do get, not the ones you don't!

Here are some tips to help you sleep better and longer:

Take your TV, cell phone, and computer out of your bedroom.
Research shows that watching TV is not relaxing. Your brain needs to work through everything it sees and doesn't rest.

Don't work in bed.
A bed is a place for relaxation and love, nothing else!

Make sure it's dark.
Melatonin, our tiredness hormone, is regulated by light and dark. Light from computer screens and cell phones comes through our eyes to our brains and disturbs the building of melatonin.

Invest in a good bed.
A good bed is a better investment than an expensive car!

Caffeine, nicotine, alcohol, and sugar can keep you awake if you consume them too close to going to bed.

Make sure your bedroom has a cool temperature.
Open the window and air out your room before you go to bed, or sleep with the window open.

Think through your problems in the daytime.
If you have problems to solve when you go to bed, write them down and decide to deal with them another day.

Exercise.
Regular exercise improves the quality of your sleep. Try not to work out just before going to bed because you can feel more awake right after training.

If you can't sleep, get up.
Do something that makes you tired, like reading a book. This gives your body another chance to start the falling asleep process when you lie down again.

Don't eat right before going to bed.
You won't sleep well with a full stomach but, at the same time, you shouldn't go to bed hungry.

Try to maintain a regular sleeping schedule.
Decide when you will go to bed and wake up and try to stick to those times every day. Going to bed before ten p.m. is a good rule of thumb.

Try to wind down for a while before you go to bed.
If you have a chance, do a relaxation exercise.

Make a ritual out of going to bed.
Do the same thing every evening - for example put on some body lotion, read a chapter of a book, and brush your teeth. After a few weeks your body will know when it's time to sleep.

Try not to sleep during the day.
Wake up later and go to bed earlier if nothing else helps.

> **"Let her sleep. For when she wakes up, she will move mountains."**
>
> **Anonymous**

RELAXATION EXERCISE

Here is a good exercise to use if you have a hard time falling asleep, or wake up in the middle of the night and have a hard time going back to sleep:

- If it's possible, lie on your back with your arms at your sides and your hands at your sides or on your stomach. Legs should be straight and still. You can also place a pillow or a rolled up blanket under your knees if it feels uncomfortable in your lower back. Close your eyes.

- Focus on your chest and belly. Notice how they rise and fall with every breath.

- Breathe calmly, in and out through your nose. Count your breaths as you exhale from one to ten, for example: In, Out - one. In,

Out - two. In, out - three etc. Then count your breaths backwards from ten to one. Repeat from the beginning.

If you get distracted by your thoughts and lose count, just start over.

This exercise helps you learn to break up your thoughts, relax in your body, and focus on what's happening right now.

"The day is over, night has come.
Today is gone, what's done is done.
Embrace your dreams, through
the night. Tomorrow comes with a
whole new light."

Anonymous

TO MEDICATE OR NOT?

Antidepressants (SSRI's) are medicines meant to, in part, help you get to a mental state where you can change your lifestyle and your negative behaviors.

Many people who suffer from stress and anxiety wonder if they should medicate. If you feel like you need medicine this does not mean you are weak or a lost cause. It's nothing to be ashamed of. It also doesn't mean you have to take medicine for the rest of your life.

If you are going to medicate, you should start seeing a therapist or psychologist at the same time, preferably one specialized in cognitive behavioral therapy.

Cognitive behavioral therapy (CBT) is a psychotherapeutic treatment. CBT teaches you to replace the thoughts, feelings, and behaviors that contribute to your mental illness. It helps you to get rid of your symptoms and prevent them from returning. CBT is a structured, active, and enlightening form of psychotherapy that focuses more on the present and future than the past.

LET MEDICINE BE A SUPPORT

Antidepressants can help you to feel calmer, feel more balanced, and soften otherwise intense reactions. Be aware that it can take several weeks before they start to make a difference, and they may, in the beginning, even worsen your fear and anxiety.

If you instead decide to try an anxiety-reducing medication like Oxazepam, Valium, or Xanax, be mindful that they are addictive. These medications should, therefore, only be taken for a short period of time and in limited amounts. Consult with your doctor, therapist, or psychologist about what is best for you.

Antidepressants do not help everyone. Some people's symptoms can even worsen. Others may have to try out a few different medications before they find an antidepressant that works for them.

> **Our Experiences:**
> *I, Mats, was vehemently against medication from the beginning (which is typical of anxious people). I was deathly afraid of the side-effects and the risk of addiction. But once I was at my lowest point and could barely function in everyday life, I didn't have a choice. I started to take an antidepressant and it gave me relief from my anxiety so that I could more easily benefit from the therapy I had just started.*
>
> *I, Susan, also took an antidepressant for a period of time. The medication helped me to more easily control my intense emotional*

overreactions. I also sought help from a cognitive behavioral therapist who gave me a variety of exercises to practice. I thought it felt very good to talk to a professional and to get help with the things I could and needed to change. It is tough and even hurts to gain new insights into your behavior, but it is necessary for recovery.

STIMULANTS DON´T MAKE LIFE EASIER

Many people use different stimulants to pick themselves up, calm down, comfort themselves, or increase their self-confidence. After being used they can leave you feeling more sensitive to stress and make you feel even worse with feelings of guilt, worry, and anxiety. Dependence on these stimulants can become a harmful habit or an addiction.

We think that a cigarette, a cup of coffee, a glass of wine or a piece of chocolate will help us to relax, when in fact the exact opposite is true!

You may feel that you become alert, and yes, you will, for a little while. But then the side-effects sink in. You feel even more tired and even more anxious, and you need to "fill it up" again.

This up and down cycle continues. As the day comes to a close you can understand that your body is hurting from the "help" of the stimulant. **This creates yet another negative feeling - guilt.**

SUGAR

When we eat foods that are high in sugar, our blood sugar levels rise and produce insulin to decrease the blood sugar level. When there is too much insulin the blood sugar becomes too low. For the body to reach a normal level again it produces adrenaline. **Adrenaline has the side effect of making us more nervous, worried and full of anxiety.**

In the last few years a whole slew of new kinds of sugars and sweeteners have started to appear in our food. High fructose corn syrup, maltodextrin, dextrose, corn starch, aspartame, sucralose and stevia are just a few examples. Too much aspartame can act as a laxative. Sucralose is associated with inflammatory bowel disease. Research also shows artificial sweeteners to be associated with type 2 diabetes, heart disease, metabolic syndrome, and obesity. **The new sweeteners have the same negative effects on the body as ordinary sugars.**

Some of the new sweeteners can even be more dangerous because the body and brain cannot absorb them and use them as energy. They instead get stored in the liver which then changes them to fat.

> **Susan's Sweet-Tooth:**
> *I have had, during certain periods of time, intense sugar cravings. Trying to avoid sugar is torturous because sugar is everywhere! I tend to have cravings right after dinner. My cravings are especially strong if I eat a dinner*

rich in carbohydrates, like pasta or white bread, or if I eat fast food. The only way for me to avoid unhealthy sweets is to not have them at home. If they are there, I can't control myself. Despite the fact that science says that sugar isn't addictive, I experience myself as addicted. When I don't get sugar when I am craving it, I can become unbelievably irritable. But this is really about habits. I sometimes have fruit, cottage cheese with cinnamon and a few slices of banana. When I am really being good I just brush my teeth and it actually helps!

When Julia was little we always noticed a huge change in her behavior after eating sweets. Once a week she got to pick out some candy at the grocery store. After she ate it she became more active, whiney, and irritable, and she often wanted more candy when she ran out. Looking back, we shouldn't have given her candy at all, but denying her was difficult.

Parents today are becoming more aware of the effects of sugar and many are trying to limit their children's sugar intake. But it's not easy. A lot of products advertised for children have a lot of added sugar. Yoghurt, cereal, and juice products for children often have more sugar than similar products for adults. This is a problem because the children's bodies are small and the doses are high. It is also not good to start the day with high levels of sugar. It increases sugar cravings for the rest of the day. The Swedish government recommends not more than 1.5 deciliters of candy per week for school age children, and also recommends drinking water with meals, not softdrinks or juice.

CAFFEINE

Caffeine is found in coffee, green and black tea, chocolate and guarana. Energy drinks, have become much more popular and the consumption has increased in recent years. Many of those people drinking energy drinks are children and youths. Their small bodies can't handle the level of caffeine and they are also not as used to caffeine as an adult is. There is a high risk for them to overdose. Children can experience symptoms such as nausea, dizziness, anxiety, heart palpitations and muscle twitches. Caffeine is very stress inducing and can give symptoms such as difficulty in concentrating, nervousness, increased irritability and anxiety. Caffeine overstimulates the central nervous system.

The Swedish government recommends reducing caffeine intake for pregnant women because too much caffeine can lead to miscarriage. Caffeine can also be dangerous when mixed with alcohol. Caffeine is a stimulant and alcohol is a depressant, which means that when you combine them you do not feel the intoxication in the right way. There is a risk that too much alcohol is consumed.

ALCOHOL

Alcohol has become an extremely socially accepted drug in our society. Choosing not to drink in different social situations can be thought of as suspicious behaviour. In fact, alcohol can easily become an addiction. Alcoholism is a complicated illness and people who have it often needs help to deal with it. Many people drink as a way to wind down or relax. The limits for what is over consumption are not always so easy to see.

Alcohol can both sedate and amplify emotions. Over time it increases feelings of guilt and anxiety. It also increases appetite, is high in calories, and strengthens sugar cravings. Don't be afraid to get professional help if you feel that you are on the edge of over consumption!

CRAVINGS AND HABITS DRIVE YOUR LIFE

It is possible to weaken and even end your cravings for sugar, coffee, cigarettes, and alcohol. Part of you knows you shouldn't take that piece of candy, cigarette, or glass of wine, but you do it anyway. Why? Because the signals that your body gives that you should stop are too difficult to handle. We simply don't want to listen to our bodies.

There is, of course, a reason why you overconsume something. Maybe you want comfort, escape, or relaxation. Maybe you're looking to fill the emptiness inside you. All stimulants give some type of reward. If your reward from alcohol is relaxation, find a healthier way to unwind. If caffeine picks you up but you want to end the habit, take a brisk walk instead!

Always try to find a healthy alternative that gives you the same or better rewards.

Often when we feel a craving coming on, we just try to repress it. But the more we try not to think about it, the more afraid we get that we will fail to repress it. Then it becomes even harder to handle the craving.

Instead of trying to ignore or repress your craving, listen to it. Pay attention. How do you feel when you feel the craving coming on? What are you thinking? Are you blaming yourself? **Do you try to convince yourself that it's not such a big deal if you give in just this once?**

WHEN CRAVINGS COME

Think about all the positive things that will come if you DON'T give in to your craving.

Decide to wait ten minutes before you give in. Pay attention to how it feels to hold back during that time.

Observe and describe your feelings. It's okay to feel whatever you feel. You will notice that it isn't so frightening.

Embrace the feeling, not the impulse to do something that you don't want to do. If you become restless, do something to keep busy. Take a walk, work, or call someone. If you feel tired, lie down for a while or take a nap. **Notice how long it takes for the craving to go away.**

The more you practice not giving in, the easier it will get. Your life will be better if you manage to endure it until the impulse and craving disappear.

You will feel stronger.

In the future when you feel that your stress and anxiety have gotten better or disappeared, you can obviously let yourself have a coffee, tea, glass of wine, or piece of chocolate. But if you have had a damaging habit or addiction to one of these substances, then it's probably best for you to avoid any consumption in the future.

Most important when it comes to these substances is that you become conscious of how they influence you and where your limits are.

COLOR AND FORM - FOR WELLBEING

We may know what colors we like and don't like, but not too many people think about how colors influence them. In nature color always has a meaning. Plants which need to attract insects for their survival are often very bright in color.

The most common favorite color in the world is blue. Maybe this is because we can all relate to it because the sky is blue. Our lips are red so we can get our hormones and sexual going. Women's nipples are reddish-brown so that newborns can find their food.

India used color as therapy as early as 2000 B.C. Egyptians were also early in using color in a therapeutic way.

Karl Ryberg, architect and psychologist, writes in his book, Colors in Everyday Life and Therapy:

> *Countless medical studies have been done to learn about the effects of color and light on our organism. The results show that color has a strong influence on our body's homeostasis, or balance. Colored lights can have a variety of*

physiological impacts depending on frequency and color. Many of these effects occur even if subjects cannot see the lights or colors with their eyes. The pineal gland and pituitary gland react to the light flow and releases hormones. These responses are not only determined by light that reaches our eyes, but even by light that touches our skin. This is worth thinking about because it points to the fact that our whole body is a light receptor with a primitive "total seeing", much like a worm or a larva. Some light experiments are done by nature itself: In extreme northern latitudes, Inuit women's menstruation stops during the darkest months of winter, resulting in temporary sterility. In contrast, tropical women are fertile year round despite starvation levels of food, and hardship.

Colors are vibrations. The stronger the color, the stronger the vibrations. These vibrations allow us to perceive colors not only with our eyes, but through our skin! That is why blind people can perceive colors.

Feelings, thoughts, blood pressure, body temperature, breathing and immune response are influenced by colors.

Colored light is healing. Blue light, for example, is used the world over for infants born with jaundice! You can also use colors everyday to stimulate your wellbeing.

Below is a little explanation about how different colors influence us and how they are perceived.

RED

Red influences the nervous system and thereby increases the secretion of adrenaline. Blood pressure, breathing, and blood sugar levels rise. Sex hormones are activated and muscle strength is increased. Red is the color of blood and fire. We experience warmth; we feel enthusiastic and active. Red is associated with love, passion, desire, energy, war, danger, strength, power and decisiveness and can therefore can be experienced as worrisome and stressful in some people. In the U.S. people with red sports cars are charged higher accident insurance rates than others: statistics prove that drivers of red sports cars take crazier risks than others and cause more accidents.

BLUE

Blue has the opposite effect on our nervous system as red. Blue leads the adrenal gland to secrete cortisole, which lowers blood pressure, slows breathing, and lowers adrenaline levels. Blue increases oxygen levels in the body, reduces hormonal activity, and reduces inflammation. We experience blue as calming but also a little depressing. It is a good color for the room of a hyperactive child. Blue is associated with awareness and intellect. Blue is seen as trustworthy, reliable, and faithful. Dark blue is associated with wealth and power.

YELLOW

Yellow is said to increase the level of alertness and is mentally stimulating because it is the color of the sun. Yellow is understood to express optimism, enlightenment, happiness, luck, intellect and energy.

People with reading difficulties are said to be helped by having yellow walls and reading text on a yellow background. Yellow is a spontaneous and unstable color.

GREEN

Green is seen as a very neutral color. It is calming, relaxing, and is generally perceived as a pleasant color associated with harmony, youth and freshness. Green stimulates development, growth, fertility, stability, and endurance. Green aids concentration and makes us feel safe.

ORANGE

Orange improves circulation and is associated with both strong positive and negative feelings. It represents enthusiasm, fascination, happiness, creativity, determination, attraction, success, encouragement and stimulation. Orange increases appetite and stimulates digestion. In Christianity it represents gluttony.

PURPLE/VIOLET

Purple combines the stability of the cold color blue and with the warm color red. Purple is associated with wisdom, dignity, independence, creativity, mystery, magic, strength, nobility, luxury, royalty and ambition. It is inspiring and increases creativity.

PINK

Pink is generally a weaker version of what the red color generates and is associated with. It symbolizes love and affection but not passion! Pink is stimulating for girls and calming for boys. A particular shade - Miller pink - is so calming that many police stations in the U.S. have

Miller Pink rooms where they put violent suspects to calm them down.

BROWN

Brown expresses stability, reliability and approachability. It denotes masculine qualities. Brown is the color of the earth, of our origins. It is associated with all things natural and organic. We may also experience it as dirty.

BLACK

Black devours energy and is experienced as still, quiet, and heavy. Black can be associated with strength, authority, elegance, death, evil, and mystery. Black is considered a very formal and prestigious color. Too much black creates depression and makes people feel ill at ease. Black can also be used in contrast to accentuate objects and in small doses to create tension and dynamics.

WHITE

White is associated with light, goodness, peace, innocence, cleanliness, neutrality, easiness and safety. White is the color that gets the other colors to stand out more clearly. Too much white can be experienced as cold and sterile.

GREY

Grey is the color of intellect, knowledge, and wisdom. It is dignified, conservative, and authoritative. Grey is controlled, almost unremarkable and the color of compromise, and can be associated with self-restraint and independence.

Colors symbolize different things in different cultures. In Sweden, for example, we decorate our houses with red for Christmas when it is freezing to bring a warmer cosy feeling. We decorate our bathrooms with blue, green, and white to make them feel fresh and clean. We have an intuitive feeling for using colors to create balance, if we only dare to listen to our feelings. It's no coincidence that banks use blue in their logos or that men often choose dark blue suits. It is easy to understand why fire trucks are red. We are constantly influenced by color composition, consciously and subconsciously.

Dark colors make things seem smaller and light colors make things seem bigger. Dark colors seem heavy and light colors seem more airy. With this knowledge you can change and create your surroundings and yourself to suit your moods and your self-presentation.

Our home:
We have created a pretty colorful home for ourselves. It is possible that some people think it's too much. We have held ourselves to a yellow, red, and orange color scheme on the first floor where the living room and kitchen are. On the second floor we have two bedrooms and an office. These rooms are blue, pink, and purple, which are calming and at the same time stimulating. The stairs between the floors are grey-striped to be neutralizing.

We have had the same color scheme for 13 years and we are still happy with it. Our 18-year-old daughter Julia, however, would probably like a change. She has grown up surrounded by color and has a need, like all other teenagers, to do things differently from her parents. Recently she decided to paint the walls of her room in white and beige.

Many people don't even take the time to think about how they want things to be. They don't dare to do what they want and instead copy their neighbours, friends or home decorating magazines. This is a shame, because the people behind those home decorating magazines want you to buy new things and replace them often. When we follow trends, we tire of them more quickly because we haven't thought about how we really want things to be. Maybe then we wouldn't feel such a great desire to change things so often. Dare to do what feels right for you!

FORMS

Can shapes in nature, our homes, and our furniture influence how we feel? When I talk about shape I also mean the lines surrounding us. We are influenced differently by horizontal, vertical, slanted, straight, parallel or crossing lines. We experience horizontal lines as calming. By using the lines built from the placement of your furniture, floor planks, shelves, carpets, and curtains, you can make a room feel bigger, smaller, taller, shorter or rounder. Round and oval shapes feel softer and more pleasant than ones with hard edges and corners. Perfectly straight lines and angles are not found in nature. The lines and shapes most common in nature make us feel the best.

Architect and researcher Alan Dilani of the Center for Psychosocial Medicine in Solna gave an interesting interview in the newspaper Barometern. He said, among other things:

> *Well thought-out architecture and design creates feelings of coherence and safety, so that the environment becomes psychosocially supportive for wellness. If we create harmonious spaces both in terms of clearness shape, color, material, air and light; and build places where people naturally gather and make sure that they can withdraw and be alone; then we support health. There is much research to show that attractive environments lower blood pressure, strengthen the immune system, calm our heart rhythm, decrease stress and depression and reduce the need for pain relieving medications.*
>
> *Good architecture also increases creativity, stimulates passion, and makes us happy.*
>
> *[...] So much research nowadays shows that with small but well thought out means we can prevent a lot of sickness. [...] Our health care system only accounts for about 10 per cent of that which creates our health. Lifestyle,*

e.g. recreation and activity in our living and work environment, accounts for about 50 per cent. The environment we live in accounts for about 20 per cent, and the remaining 20 per cent is dependent upon genes, according to research from Ingmar Norling at Sahlgrenska University.

Isn't it nice to know that only 20 per cent of our health is dependent upon genetics? The other 80 per cent we can more or less influence.

In sum, what makes us feel better is:

- Harmony and balance in the placement of furniture, paintings, fabrics, and sources of light.
- Clear/well arranged spaces and rooms.
- Natural patterns and materials that give comfortable associations such as wood, bamboo, grass, seashells, stone, glass, metals, natural fabrics and sheepskin.
- Lots of light, especially daylight.
- Soft lighting, preferably many small light sources as opposed to a few big ones. Candle light also creates an atmosphere.
- Water. It is calming and gives moisture to the dry air inside of houses.

- Furniture to sit on and beds placed so that you can see the door, the bed not placed under the window.
- Colors that you like, not just colors that are trendy right now.
- Paintings, pictures, photos and other decorative items that mean something to us.
- Living plants. They make a room feel cosy, and we have a feeling of being in nature. Potted plants make the air more humid and make it easier to breathe. Plants also remove chemicals and toxins from the air. Some good air purifying plants are: Gerbera, Common ivy, Cornstalk dracaena, Peace lily, and Dracaena marginata.

CREATING HEALTH

In history there was no distinction made between artistic and everyday activities like there is today. The Sami people, the indigenous people of northern Scandinavia, even have a word for this: Duodji. The word simultaneously means handicraft, the Sami lifestyle and the attitude to nature and man. Art used to be integrated into all aspects of life, including hunting, cooking, creating necessary items, and clothes. Art was also part of communication, conflict solving, healing and medicinal practices. Only in the last centuries has art been seen as a special process separate from our daily lives. This is not a good thing because it splits people instead of uniting them.

Susan´s Healing:
The first thing I did in my exhaustion depression sick leave was to sleep. I was excessively tired and had had aches in certain areas of my body for many years. Sharp pains came and went like arrow shots in different places in my body. I slept when Mats and Julia left in the morning and I was still asleep when they came back in the evening. After six months of sleeping the pain was gone! I then started to

go to cognitive behavioral therapy and I forced myself to start taking walks. I have always enjoyed being in the forest. I love the scents, the sounds, the quiet and the stillness, and I often take a piece of nature home with me. In the spring of 2002 I picked some birch twigs to make a wreath to hang from the ceiling. I took out some tongs and steel wire and started to weave the birch. (As I am writing this I begin to cry because this became such an important breakthrough for me). There and then my passion woke up! I didn't understand right away what was happening, and it took a long time for everything to fall into place. I couldn't name exactly what was happening to me. What I did with my hands gave me new life! Now I understand how strong this healing through creativity was for my recovery.

I continued experimenting with steel wire. This led me to take up wire handicraft. Then wool came into my life through a teacher in Julia's preschool. Thank you wonderful Gunilla! I love to combine the unexpected materials. Nowadays I do a lot of upcycling from old materials, with diversity in materials and contrast as the driving forces in my creation. To be able to create has been a way for me live and survive!

NEW RESEARCH AND NEW EXPERIMENTS

Recently there has been much research done into how creativity and cultural activities influence how we feel. The media reported that dancing, singing in choirs, and even theater should be written as prescriptions.

Brain researcher Dr. Pontus Wasling writes in his book Memory Back and Forth:

> *One study from Finnish Osterbotten shows how important social life is. The population there is a mixture of Swedish- and Finnish-speaking people, and there is a large difference in heart disease mortality rates between the two groups. This despite the fact that they have the same genetic background, the same smoking habits, the same physical activity, and the same eating and alcohol habits. The difference in mortality rates is explained by social cohesion. The Swedish group has stronger social connections than the Finnish group, and that is enough to give them healthier and longer lives. One explanation for the greater social connection is that the Swedish speakers more often sing in choirs.*

There is even research into how we can use cultural activities during working hours to reduce sick leave. Studies have been done with "free days" at, among other places, Google's head office in LA. Employees get to pick one day each week to do whatever they want.

These “free days” resulted in increased creativity and self-discipline which led to improved performance, and greater productivity while at work.

> **“True art is characterized by an irresistible urge in the creative artist.”**
> **Albert Einstein**

Today we know, through research, how cultural activities affect the body. Eva Boijner Horwitz describes some of these impacts in her fantastic book Culture for Health’s Sake. In the book she describes 16 different cultural and recreational activities, what parts of the body they affect, and what kind of health-promoting effects they have. **How fantastic that we can reduce our stress hormones through knitting!** That we can improve our muscle memory through dance and strengthen our immune system when we write!

WHAT HAPPENS IN THE BRAIN AND BODY?

Simply put, the brain’s neurons are connected through something called synapses. We use our synapses to work through and store all of our thoughts and feelings, but they must constantly be stimulated to survive. When we practice cultural activities our brain becomes more plastic, meaning the number of synapses increases and new memory cells are created. Today it is even possible to use special cameras to measure how the brain responds to different cultural activities. Some activities strengthen synapses’ resilience. When activities increase and are strengthened in the synapses we more easily gain access to our memories, thoughts, and feelings. It makes us feel better.

When we practice different artistic and cultural activities we get to know our body better, our stress hormones decrease, we strengthen our immune system, our blood pressure goes down, we work through our feelings, and we feel calmer.

When we create something concrete that we can see and feel, **we become more present in the moment, we have a feeling of connection,** we relax, we feel more energetic, we become braver and it becomes easier to break bad habits ... and much more! Horwitz continues:

> *Creating through listening or doing strikes a holy chord that affects us deeply. Creating challenges us by pushing us outside our boundaries, and inspires us with new knowledge. This is what gives artistic and cultural activities both spiritual and healing effects.*
>
> *[…] The collaboration between the mind, the nervous system, and immune system explains part of the healing effects of art. […] The strength of mental ideas/conceptions can change physical processes in the body and thereby are seen as healing! […] We try to supplement feelings we can't put into words with the help of symbols. However, these symbols can't replace the body's own symbols and forms of*

expression. Cultural activities can, to a certain degree, fulfil these non-verbal and wordless aspects that we need to create a feeling of completeness and wellness.

What is needed for it to be health-promoting?
The activity should be done voluntarily. It should make you feel passion and pleasure.

What is a creative activity?
Creative activities include building something new, making something new of something old, using your imagination or role play. Children's fantasy games and role play are very important for their creative development. Activities with lots of rules, competition, and imitation, or activities that are purely functional (biking, walking), are less creative. Giving rewards is not a good way of stimulating the creative process.

> **"All children are artists. The problem is how to remain an artist when once he grows up."**
>
> **Pablo Picasso**

How is an idea born?
Dr. Pontus Wasling explains the general structure of memory in Memory Back and Forth. He writes about two types of memory that use different parts of the brain. One type is the "I-know-that" (convergent) memory by which you realize that something can be done; and the other is the "I-know-how"

(divergent) memory, by which you grasp the method to accomplish it. We must combine convergent and divergent memories to create a new idea. But there is more needed to become creative than just this.

HOW CAN YOU BECOME MORE CREATIVE?

One step you can take is to improve your divergent thinking, to practice learning HOW things work. One classic creativity exercise that you may recognize is to give a person or a group a paper clip, a safety pin, a chair, or some other mundane object and ask them to come up with as many uses for it as possible. Another one is to add the word "not" in a question. A third is to ask how many different number combinations they can think of that add up to 8, instead of just asking what four plus four is.

Here are good exercises for a group or individual to practice to begin to think outside the box:

If you want to become more creative:

- Take silent breaks.
- Make connections between things. Put together "I-know-that" with "I-know-how."
- Remember to reflect and summarize.
- Dare to fail.
- Move yourself! Change place, room or take a trip somewhere.
- When you get stuck, stop and do something else.

- Think in opposites.
- Do something you've never done before.

Why is it good to increase your creativity and practice cultural activities?

Creativity is not only important in art. We all need to be creative every day. We need it when we make decisions, when we solve problems, communicate with others, and when we deal with our children and other adults.

When we are more creative we feel that things become more manageable and we feel more comfortable and safe.

One thing that distinguishes creative people is that they are much more open and have a higher tolerance level. Isn't this a quality we need more of these days?

"Creativity is intelligence having fun."

Albert Einstein

CHANGES AND HABITS

"I may not be where I need to be, but thank God I'm not where I used to be."
Joyce Meyer

When we feel internally unstable, the need for habits, correctness and routines takes on extra importance. When there is chaos in our brains we often try to compensate with stable surroundings.

Intuitively we always seek balance.

Everything we know and do we have copied from people in our environment, learned through repetition and created habits. Good habits and bad habits. The good habits strengthen us and the bad habits make us feel worse. Familiar things make us feel safe and secure. Even something negative can feel safe because we are used to it.

We easily get stuck in our habits and opinions and fight tooth and nail for them. The solution when you don't feel good is change.

Change is needed to break old bad habits and replace them with new, healthy ones that make you feel good!

Our brain hates change. It takes three or four weeks to create a new habit, under the condition that we repeat it as much as necessary. It also depends on what we want to change. Anyone who has tried to break a habit knows that it can take a long time and that it can be tough. You need to gather a lot of strength and courage. You might also need help from your family, a friend, or even a therapist.

It can be hard to remember that a pattern needs to be broken and that something needs to be done in a different way. Write reminders on your hands, put up notes, and ask people around you to remind you.

A major reason as to why you have one or more bad habits is that they come with rewards, even though the reward is not good for you!

> **"You must learn a new way to think before you can master a new way to be."**
>
> **Marianne Williamson**

Though it may sound strange, even when it comes to stress, worry and anxiety, we can get stuck in a bad behavior because of its payoffs. Many people fight against getting better because they have gotten used to the positive effects, because they do exist, even if you may not believe that they do.

Lucinda Bassett tells an interesting story:

> *A truck driver contacted me after completing one of my anti-anxiety courses. He said the program hadn't helped him at all. I asked him how he felt about driving a truck. "I hate it!" he said. I asked him how he supported himself. "I am on sick leave."*

No wonder he didn't get better! His reward for his illness was to avoid going to a job he hated.

In order to create a new habit it needs to be followed by a reward! When you want to break a bad habit and replace it with a good one, you need to replace the reward system in your brain with something as least as good as the reward you are trying to replace.

Sit down in peace and quiet and write down the rewards you have for remaining in your negative behaviors. **You need to be honest with yourself.**

Maybe you will find that you get more attention from people when you're not feeling well. Maybe you get out of obligations and responsibilities because the people around you are taking care of you. Maybe you're not expected to help out as much at home because your family feels sorry for you.

Your sickness can also be an excuse for you to avoid doing important things like changing jobs, getting out of a bad relationship, etc.

It is easy to blame others, especially if you grew up in

a divided family with different problems. Try to accept the past. Try to forgive yourself and others for what has happened and get on with your life. You may need help from a therapist.

It can feel scary to know that you have responsibility for your own life. But that level of fear can turn into the same level of pleasure when you take control of your life! When you decide to make positive changes you will grow as a person!

The benefits of change and recovery are much more compelling than the limited rewards you get by using negative attitudes as an excuse!

You need to take responsibility for yourself and stop blaming others. Realize that it is you who decides if you are going to make the changes needed to minimize your stress, worry or other negative behaviors.

> **"Change and growth take place when a person has risked himself and dares to become involved with experimenting with his own life."**
>
> **Herbert Otto**

We've all heard the excuses. "I can't change." "I am what I am." "You know me." "It is my style." "It's always been this way" etc. These are the same as saying that they don't want to change, showing that they are afraid of change. **It shows that they are saying no to growing and developing as a person!**

Imagine that life is like a big present with many small presents inside. You haven't opened all the packages yet. Your resistance to change prevents your curiosity from revealing what is in the rest of the packages. Once you start to open several packages you will find that they are unlimited! Not opening your presents is like preventing your own development towards a better life!

Don't put things off until tomorrow, until you are healthier or until someone else takes the initiative. Life is too short for things to be put off to the future. **Try to live more in the now.**

The following wonderful excerpt is from Living, Loving, Learning by Leo F. Buscaglia:

> *"To laugh is to risk appearing the fool." Well, so what? Fools have a lot of fun.*
>
> *"To weep is to risk being called sentimental." Of course I'm sentimental. I love it! Tears can help.*
>
> *"To reach out to another is to risk involvement." Who's risking involvement? I want to be involved.*
>
> *"To expose feelings is to risk showing your true self." What else do I have to show?*
>
> *"To place your ideas and your dreams before the crowd is to risk being called naive." Oh, I'm called worse things than that.*

"To love is to risk not being loved in return." I don't love to be loved in return.

"To live is to risk dying." I'm ready for it. Don't you dare shed one tear if you hear that Buscaglia blew up in the air or dropped dead. He did it with enthusiasm.

"To hope is to risk despair, and to try is to risk failure." But risks must be taken, because the greatest risk in life is to risk nothing. The person who risks nothing, does nothing, has nothing, is nothing, and becomes nothing. He may avoid suffering and sorrow, but he simply cannot learn and feel and change and grow and love and live. Chained by his certitudes, he's a slave. He's forfeited his freedom. Only the person who risks is truly free. Try it and see what happens.

It is about daring to take risks in life.

This is what life is all about.

ENERGY THIEVES

You are probably wondering how people in your surroundings will react when you begin to change yourself and your life. They will probably react positively and treat you with a new respect when you dare to stand up for yourself and prioritize your needs. Those who don't, are probably having difficulty handling your changes because of jealousy or dissatisfaction with their own inability to change. You can manage without these people in your life: they don't bring anything positive but instead will only drain your energy. They might think it was better before you changed. They may feel you might suddenly say things they aren't used to hearing you say. You may do things you haven't done before. They can feel that you have become selfish because you may suddenly say no and dare to set boundaries.

Surround yourself with people who want you to feel good.

You need to ask yourself who benefits the most from your changes.

Changes should start within you, in your way of thinking, reacting, and relating to others. How do you let your environment influence you?

How do you see yourself and your opportunities? It is important to know what you want and that you can stand up for what you do so you can reach your goals - because they are YOURS and nobody else's!

Every day is a new day and YOU decide how you want to experience it.

No changes happen without hard work. The only thing you need to get started is the knowledge that YOU create your life if you want to, otherwise other people will do it for you! It's not easy to maintain your originality when the rest of society is all about making us copies of each other.

Mats' Excuses:

I asked myself what I gained from my stress, worry and anxiety. I could only admit to how they hurt me. Today I see them clearly! I didn't have to take much practical responsibility at home. I got out of cleaning the house, doing laundry, and making food, since Susan was home on maternity leave anyway! Susan didn't want to ask for my help when she saw how stressed, tired, and worn down I was when I came home. I always had one excuse or another about why I didn't have time to exercise. In truth it was laziness and that I did not prioritize my body. I was uncomfortable when I was supposed to go to the gym because I thought that everyone there was in much better shape than I was. But once I forced myself into going, despite being tired and busy, I felt what an enormous good training did to relieve my stress and anxiety.

Now exercise has become a positive habit for me. There is nothing that can stop me from exercising.

Susan's Negative Behavior:

As a young woman I had a negative behaviour that expressed itself as, among other things, aggression. Apparently I was rewarded for my aggression because it got me my own way. Not that I was lazy: I always worked hard, tried to do everything myself and liked to make decisions. I worked hard to get praise. I wanted to be heard and ventilate my opinions constantly so that I wouldn't seem shallow, gloomy, ignorant, boring etc. I was afraid of not being liked because, in fact, I was a person with very low self-esteem. The rewards I received from this behavior have become clearer to me. Today I have worked to change this behaviour a little at a time. I have realized that I can be liked for reasons other than my performance.

As a couple and as a family, we have made a number of changes to "come back" and live a more satisfying life. One change we felt was very important to make was to stop working so much. To do this, we had to lower our expenses. We sold our large house and bought a smaller, cheaper condo. We sold one car and reviewed our other costs to see where cuts could be made.

We have made many changes to create a better quality of life. We have changed our eating habits and make more healthy choices when cooking. We talk to each other more and we try to eat together every evening in the kitchen for a quiet peaceful meal. This is when we share what happened during the day. Everyone has a chance to reflect and see each other and not just run past each other. We try to have cell-phone free dinners.

Open your mind and let yourself be drawn into the exciting journey leading to change and creating new positive habits. Open all those exciting new presents - they are just lying there waiting for you!

"If we all go in the same direction we will never meet!"

Anonymous

YOU DESERVE TO FEEL WELL!

> **"Enjoy the small things in life. One day you might look back and realize that the small things were not small at all."**
>
> **Anonymous**

Do you feel that this has this been a lot to take in? Our hope is that this book will get you to start reflecting over where you are in your life.

Start by thinking about what is good in your life and write it down. Thankfulness is good for the soul!

Then write down the not so good.

When you do this you will find the reasons why you want to change your situation and at the same time find the motivation.

With the help of the tips, advice, and techniques described in this book, you can begin your transformation into someone able to reach their goals.

So much of your transformation centers on the way you choose to think. What do you choose to focus on? Do you choose that which is negative and hard in your everyday or the positive things that bring you joy? It's your choice - no one else can choose for you! Your stress and worry are caused largely by your way of thinking. It is never too late to change. Even if you never learned what was important to focus upon during your childhood, you can still learn it today.

If you find that the knowledge and advice found in this book are not enough to help you, don't hesitate to contact a doctor. Be open and clear about what your feelings and symptoms are. Once you have taken these first steps, you will feel a great relief and your change can begin. We know it can be done. You are not alone.

There is a lot of positive energy and power in all people. Some of us just need help finding it.

You deserve to feel well and you can change!

There is always something to be thankful for!

> **"When you FORGIVE, you don't change the PAST.**
> **You change the FUTURE!"**
> **Anonymous**

MATS AND SUSAN TODAY

Today we understand how important it is to think in a more positive and realistic way. We remind each other every day so we don't forget. We pay more attention to our bodies; we notice how they react when we don't take good care of ourselves. We take these signs seriously and try as soon as possible to behave in a healthier way.

Today we dare to say no, we have more realistic expectations, we have learned to stand for what we believe in and we have become better at accepting and liking ourselves.

We now prioritize ourselves because we know that it helps our entire family. We have a greater respect for each other and we listen more to each other's opinions.

We remind ourselves what is important in life: that we have each other, that we have our daughter Julia, our part-time foster children Elsa and Martin, and our parents and siblings. We remind ourselves that we are healthy and how good we have it. We try our best to encourage, praise, and take better care of each other.

We try to remind each other every day to be more present in the now. It's easier to remember since we're both striving for the same goal.

Today we run a company called Inner Health Education near Kalmar, Sweden. In a beautiful 19th century house we have an office, studio, boutique, and teaching spaces. We engage in individual and pair coaching.

> **"Make conscious presence a natural part of your life. It will change your whole existence."**
>
> **Mats and Susan Billmark**

WE WANT TO THANK

Writing this book was a big undertaking. We are so thankful for all the help we've had from friends and family. They have given us so much support, advice, knowledge, and inspiration. Without you all we would never have been able to finish this book.

We especially want to thank...

Mathias Billmark, for your ideas and patience. Thanks to your knowledge and your help this book became what we wanted it to be.

Gun Dombrowsky Nilsson, for your carefulness, and for your understanding of our writing.

Eva and Stig Sjöde, for your support during our most difficult time. Without this fantastic couple we wouldn't be together today.

Julia Billmark, for having such patience for mom and dad and all of our special projects.

Ulla Billmark, for taking care of Alice, our dog, when we didn't have time, and for taking care of the little things that mean so much.

Mikael Werthwein, for your engagement and your

enthusiasm. You are a true friend. It has been so wonderful to be able to bounce ideas off of you during the journey. Thanks for everything you have painted and fixed for us.

Pelle Friberg, our handy man who was always there to help us with all our technical difficulties, whether it was putting together a bookshelf or helping us with IT support.

Per Eriksson, our accountant, for believing in our ideas from day one.

Olof Enström, Yves Troendlé and **Ronald Rosengren**, for your sharp eye and your quickness in checking for typos.

Carolyn Dickman, Lucinda Bassett's CEO, for your unexpected and inspiring letter.

Ylva Ellenby, for many pleasant conversations and for your good advice.

Inga-Lill Morén-Hübbinette, our doctor, for understanding the severity of our illnesses.

Tomas "Ironman" Gustavsson, for believing in us and supporting our project.

Jiri Svensson, Mats' psychologist. I couldn't have had a more qualified and knowledgeable cognitive therapist.

Kåre Wahlberg, the wonderful landlord of our little house on Öland, where we wrote this book.

EPILOGUE

During the years when we were not well, and even all the years after that, we have allowed ourselves to be inspired by many wise people. All the books we have read, all the films we have seen and all the lectures that we have been to, have - of course, left their mark within us and affected us. We have taken notes and written down all the things that we believed were smart and worth remembering. At the time we didn't believe that all we wrote down to use for our own development would later be wisdom that we would want to share in this book. We have, therefore, not always written down where everything has come from or who has said what. The sources can, where they have not been stated, therefore be uncertain. It is our desire and hope that those who have not been specified as the creators of different texts and quotes can still feel honored and grateful that their wisdom is being passed on.

We would like to quote Marianne Hallberg who said: "People who devote their time to questions for the promotion of life tend to believe that it is more important to contribute to raising the level of consciousness than to preen the feathers of the ego. We are always gathering knowledge from each other and I look at it more like placing the pieces of the puzzle - or a relay race where the baton is a bit a piece each of us, we contribute with our own perspective and pass the baton on."

We would also like to point out that everyone is responsible for their own lives. If something wakes within you that feels hard to deal with on your own - we recommend that you search help from a doctor, psychologist, or another appropriate person in the health care area or conversational partner.

Mats & Susan

15865367R00109

Printed in Great Britain
by Amazon